LLEWELLYN'S

2023

Magical Almanac

Featuring

Astrea Taylor, Blake Octavian Blair, Charlie Rainbow Wolf,
Charlynn Walls, Chic and S. Tabatha Cicero, Daniel Pharr,
Diana Rajchel, Elizabeth Barrette, Emma Kathryn,
James Kambos, JD Walker, Kate Freuler, Kelden, Lupa,
Mhara Starling, Mickie Mueller, Mireille Blacke,
Monica Crosson, Natalie Zaman, Raechel Henderson,
Sasha Graham, Stephanie Woodfield, Suzanne Ress,
and Vernon Mahabal

Llewellyn's 2023
Magical Almanac

ISBN 978-0-7387-6394-1. Copyright © 2022 by Llewellyn Publications. All rights reserved. Printed in the United States. Llewellyn Publications is a registered trademark of Llewellyn Worldwide Ltd.

Editing and design by Lauryn Heineman
Cover illustration © Faryn Hughes
Calendar pages design by Llewellyn Art Department
Calendar pages illustrations © Fiona King

Interior illustrations: © Mara Benowitz: pages 45, 46, 92, 98, 215, 218, and 271; © Kathleen Edwards: pages 18, 23, 64, 68, 196, 241, and 244; © Wen Hsu: pages 1, 27, 30, 41, 76, 81, 101, 179, 199, 202, 221, 248, 251, and 263; © Jessica Krcmarik: pages 33, 37, 84, 89, 206, 211, 254, and 259; © Mickie Mueller: 2, 7, 50, 54, 183, 186, 222, 227, and 267; © Amber Zoellner: pages 13, 15, 59, 111, 116, 191, 192, 230, and 235

All other art by Dover Publications and Llewellyn Art Department

Special thanks to Amber Wolfe for the use of daily color and incense correspondences. For more detailed information, please see *Personal Alchemy* by Amber Wolfe.

You can order Llewellyn annuals and books from *New Worlds*, Llewellyn's catalog. To request a free copy of the catalog, call 1-877-NEW-WRLD toll-free or visit www.llewellyn.com.

Astrological data compiled and programmed by Rique Pottenger. Based on the earlier work of Neil F. Michelsen.

Llewellyn Worldwide Ltd.
2143 Wooddale Drive
Woodbury, MN 55125

Contents

Earth Magic

Air Magic

2023 Almanac

Fire Magic

Water Magic

Coloring Magic

Earth Magic

rocks in missouri

Working with Stones Found in Nature

Mickie Mueller

I know so many people with shelves, boxes, bags, jars, and bottles full of crystals and stones. Yep, I'm one of them. I love working with stones in my Witchcraft and my stones are very treasured, from the biggest crystal cluster to the smallest tumbled pieces. Some of the stones I use in my Witchcraft didn't come from a mineral show, metaphysical shop, or online boutique, and some just look like plain rocks at first glance. A closer look reveals that they are a diverse collection of textures, colors, shapes, and sizes, and each comes with a story instead of a price tag. These are rocks that I found myself or were gifted by someone else who found them in nature. For a Witch who looks at the whole world and everything in it through magical eyes, these are powerful treasures to own and work with.

There are lots of reasons to collect and work magically with rocks and stones that you find in nature. For Witches in the broom closet, what looks like an interesting rock found on a hike can be a secret magical powerhouse that you can use without raising any suspicion. A found rock is also a wonderful tool for Witches on a tight budget! Something about using a found rock in my spellwork also feels so very personal, and it awakens my inner child—as a child, I used to pick up every interesting rock I saw because I knew it must be magic! Spoiler: I was right about that, and so was your inner child with pockets full of rocks!

Another great reason to use found minerals to boost your collection is that as the Witchcraft movement grows, there are so many unethical crystal mines out there that it can be a challenge to locate stones that were gathered with thought and care toward the earth and the people employed in mining them. It's always a good idea to research and ask questions when purchasing your stones, making sure to find out about the sources and learn more about mining and human rights practices of the areas where your stones are mined. Ethical sources can cost a bit more, but they are worth it. The good news is that when you find a stone on the ground, you know exactly where it came from and the circumstances in which it was gathered.

Getting started isn't as hard as you might think. Even if you're longing for the gorgeous crystal towers your fellow Witches are showing off on their social media accounts, I promise that when the thrill of rockhounding bears fruit and you find that special piece just waiting in nature for you, your witchy heart will fill up! I think they're beautiful, magical, and inspiring. All you really need is pockets and a location to get started—and of course, your intention for the right stone to find you.

Setting Your Intention to Find a Stone

When I go out for a walk, I'm not always looking for a rock but sometimes one will catch my eye. Other times I will set an intention ahead of time that I'm looking for natural supplies for a specific magical purpose. That might be planning a spell, a sabbat celebration, some personal challenge that I'm trying to overcome, or even a specific mindset that I'm trying to nurture, so when I'm out for a walk, I set an intention to find what I need.

This is quite simple to do: as I leave the house, I simply state in my mind something like "May I be guided to find a stone to support my health" or "If there is a stone that wants to help with my protection spell, please draw my attention." I usually find a special stone when I do this, perhaps a rock with an interesting stripe down the middle, an unusual color, an interesting shape, or a bit of sparkle. Remember, this isn't the same as shopping for a crystal because, of course, you don't set out on a walk outside saying, "I need a piece of malachite for my money spell," and then expect to find a glossy green and black malachite on the sidewalk.

When working with found stones, we need to rethink how we view our correspondences and our relationships with our stones a bit. The types of minerals that are in nature will vary from one location to the next, so you're working with what is local. What you are likely to find won't be a specific classification of stone (as in rose quartz for love or labradorite for psychic abilities), but it will be an individual stone with its own specific energy that is answering your request, one that is aligned with your purpose. You'll feel drawn to it and it will feel "right" when you hold it in your hand. When using this approach, you don't necessarily need look up correspondences; you listen to it and feel the purpose of the stone.

Where to Collect Stones

You may want to start in your own yard. What you can unearth close to home can be quite surprising. I remember digging in my garden and discovering a flat, multicolored stone that had a distinct eye pattern in the middle! I had asked a particular deity to watch over my home and family the previous day, and I felt it was confirmation that we were indeed being watched over. I still have that stone to this day.

I've found stones in abandoned lots while on walks through the neighborhood, along the street, or out in nature. Do be careful not to go onto another person's property for rocks, but if it's in the street or sidewalk, that's fair game. If you're out in a protected park, it's best to check with the local ordinances, as collecting might be prohibited. Beach combing or searching along rivers and streams are some of the best ways to find interesting rocks—just be aware of who owns the land and whether it is permitted to take a rock home. Finding a spot in nature that's on public property is your best bet. You can find maps with your local Bureau of Land Management to be sure of where you are hunting.

If you would love to find some specific stones in nature, another option is to check out local "fee mining" locations where you can dig for your own stones and crystals. Some even offer panning for stones. Depending on your location, you might be surprised to learn that you could find amethyst, clear quartz, garnet, hematite, jasper, opals, and many other stones. Some kinds of stones can only be found in specific locations, such as the double-terminated quartz called Herkimer diamond, which is only found in Herkimer, New York. I know an artisan who gets jewelry supplies there. My sister and her husband once spent a day picking up Pecos diamonds right off the ground along the Pecos River valley in New Mexico. They ended up with so many that she sent me a bag full of the tiny, double-terminated, rust-colored crystals. I use them to this day in crystal grids and spells and treasure them because they were gathered with care and gifted to me with love.

If you decide to visit one of these sites, be sure to call ahead or check their websites to find out details before visiting these locations. They can tell you how much the fee is, what the rules are, and what kind of rocks you're likely to find. Also, read independent reviews so that you know you'll have a good experience. Make sure to dress comfortably and bring plenty of water and sunscreen.

No matter where you choose to look for rocks, remember to respect nature and property. Never deface, damage, or remove natural features, and leave the area at least as clean as you found it. Some people like to leave an offering when they find a special stone. You can pour water onto the earth or leave a food offering. If you leave food, it can be a small cookie or cracker—just make sure it's something that won't harm wildlife if they eat it. Sometimes instead of leaving something, I clean up the area of trash. In my area littering is sadly too common, so cleaning up trash is a wonderful way to show gratitude to nature. If you do this, be sure to be careful not to cut yourself, and use globs of hand sanitizer or wash your hands thoroughly when you're done.

Name That Stone

It's perfectly fine to work with a found stone even if you can't identify it. I know it feels weird, but I give you permission (not that you need it) to learn what the stone tells you without identifying what it's called. We humans love to name things, though, so getting curious about the stones you've picked up with your own hands is okay too.

I'll walk you through my process of identifying stones I've found in nature. Remember that rock with the eye pattern I found? To narrow it down, I did a quick internet search to learn about the most common stones are in my area. I searched "most common stones in Missouri," which is where I live, which narrowed down my search. Your local college geology department knows the rocks in your area, and they are a great resource, so I checked the MSU geology department website. I discovered that chert is common in Missouri, and my stone looked like some kind of chert from photos I found linked from their site. If you try but can't identify an interesting stone you've found on your own, some college geology departments will allow you to send them photos and the location where you found it so that students or staff can help.

Next, I looked up chert in the indexes of my Witchcraft books on minerals and found it mentioned in *The Second Book of Crystal Spells* by Ember Grant, where I read that jasper and flint are both forms of chert! Apparently, flint and chert are almost the same stone but different colors: flint is gray and chert can be shades of tan, rust, or both. Both flint and chert were used in the Stone Age to make tools for making weapons to protect the people, sparking fires for protection, cooking food, and brewing medicinal plants—these stones were very important! I found flint listed in *Cunningham's Encyclope-*

dia of Crystal, Gem, & Metal Magic as well. After I finished hitting the books, I popped back on the internet and searched "chert magical properties" and "flint magical properties" and sifted through several online stone websites. My sources all agree that both flint and chert are stones of protection, healing, emotional stability, safety, and peace. I was delighted to learn from my research that the properties that I initially felt when I unearthed it from the garden have been confirmed.

You can do this with any stone you find. When I'm crystal shopping, I always grab that little slip of paper or card that tells me about its properties, but it's so rewarding to go on that journey of discovery. After doing the work, I'll never forget the properties of that little stone and how my intuition was validated by my research!

Stones for Every Magical Purpose

There are many ways to determine how a found rock or stone may be used in your Witchcraft; as I mentioned, feeling the energy from it is one of them. There are also physical characteristics that can inform magical use as well. Some of the most obvious are shape, color, and circumstances around the find.

Rocks come in all shapes, and some are more interesting than others. I have a rock my son-in-law found and gave to me that looks just like a huge coffee bean! I keep it by my coffee station in the kitchen to impart its energy boost to every brew. You can find rocks in nature with lots of interesting shapes:

- Square rocks can be used for logic, order, and control.
- Round and oval stones may have a soothing energy and can also represent movement and harmony.
- A triangle-shaped rock might be good for magic for strength, power, and direction.
- You might find stones that are shaped roughly like an item or an animal, and such stones can be used to channel the energy of what they're shaped like. Have you ever found a stone that looks a bit like a heart? That's great for love magic. One that's flat and round like a coin would be great for money spells.
- Stones with a natural hole in them are very prized. Called holy stones or hag stones, they are good for protection magic. They're traditionally hung on the bedpost for protection against nightmares.

Stones found in nature also have different colors, although the colors are often more nuanced than their polished counterparts. You can work with found stones according to their color correspondences. Even if a stone isn't bright red but reddish, that counts as red; bluish is blue, and so on.

Colors can mean different things to different people, so feel free to listen to your own heart, but general color correspondences are a good place to start.

Red: Courage, passion, fire
Pink: Love, nurturing, releasing stress

Orange: Self-worth, luck, positivity, creativity
Yellow: Expression, personal power
Green: Growth, finances, fertility
Blue: Healing, peace, communication
Purple: Psychic ability, meditation, emotional healing
White: Full moon, luck, substitution for any color
Black: Dark moon, protection, banishing, grounding
Gray: Neutralizing a situation, setting boundaries, reversing
Brown: Stability, house and home, concentration

The location a stone is found in can also have some bearing in what kind of magic you can use it for. A stone found in the bank parking lot would be great for money. A stone found on the beach when you're having a beautiful day full of love and joy can evoke that feeling in your magic. A stone found near a certain plant or tree may share some of the energies with that plant.

I hope that you will consider bringing some found stones into your magical practice. It's a very rewarding way to expand your magical tool kit but also your intuition and knowledge. As you journey down your magical path, watch that path and see what nature brings you!

Resources

Cunningham, Scott. *Cunningham's Encyclopedia of Crystal, Gem & Metal Magic.* St. Paul, MN: Llewellyn Publications, 2002.

Geology.com. Accessed August 23, 2021. https://geology.com/.

Grant, Ember. *The Second Book of Crystal Spells: More Magical Uses for Stones, Crystals, Minerals . . . and Even Salt.* Woodbury, MN: Llewellyn Publications, 2016.

The Animist Home

Blake Octavian Blair

A good number of people who practice spirit work and earth-centered spiritualities, whether they know it by name or not, have animistic beliefs. We often assign what are termed "inanimate" objects pronouns, for example. We also refer to the "character of a home" or the "soul of a place." All these are the signs of some level of animistic belief. There is a saying among shamanic practitioners that "Everything that is is alive." Do these things ring true for you? Perhaps you live in an animist home!

So how do we define animism? You'll find readily available a number of academic and working definitions for animism. Some may agree or conflict in their philosophical nuance; however, for our purposes in discussing spirituality, in general we may say that animism is an ensouled worldview, meaning everything has a soul—not just animals (humans fit into that category), but also plants, trees, rocks, cars, houses, lamps, your ritual chalice, and the dirty dishes in your sink. (I know . . . you'll get to those.) It brings us back to that handy poetic phrase of "Everything that is is alive." Another way to put it is that all things contain life force.

Embodying the Spirit

Many people—wrongly, in my eyes—think animism is a "primitive" belief. They say it in a rather derogatory way. Many cultures that are labeled primitive were anything but. However, that is a discussion for another article! These misguided perceptions of animism are rather ironic considering how prevalent animistic beliefs are right through to modern day and are even practiced by those misguided people who think that it's a bygone way of thinking. For example, how many people get into the spirit of cheering for their favorite sports team and the trappings of its animal mascot? The mascot is emblazoned onto shirts, caps, keychains, car decals, and more and then worn and carried with talismanic fervor! My own alma mater has a much-beloved alligator mascot that even has a ritual to invoke it, taking one's arms and making chomping motions like the jaws of the alligator.

Another readily available example of animistic thought in modern times is automobiles, specifically how they are named. Like sports teams, car manufacturers adopt animal spirits that evoke the qualities they want to parallel in the performance and appearance of the automobile. The sleek, smooth, and exotic nature of the jaguar. The speed and power of the mustang. The compact efficiency of the beetle. The rugged durability of a bronco. We also tend to give personal names to our automobiles along with their own pronouns. Perhaps you'll remember Aunt Betty remarking to you, "We have to take Henrietta Hatchback to the gas station. She only has an eighth of a tank of gas!"

Of course, we have long inherently understood the ensouled nature of, well, nature. The weather serves a perfect example, as we name hurricanes and long remember the feisty personalities of such raucous storms, whether they be an Andrew, Sandy, Hugo, or Francis. We also assign names to mountains, whether they be named after someone or someplace or given a more totemic name due to their characteristics. Many mountains were given names by Indigenous peoples but then later renamed by colonists. You'll often find, after some research, that the Indigenous names were far more descriptive and likely to fit the spirit of the place.

Many of us also, in a more microcosmic view, live in animist homes. Whether conscious or unconscious of what we are doing, we speak of where the TV remote, the kitchen toaster, or the sewing box "lives." The items have homes. Many even have names and personalities. Do you play an instrument that has a name? Perhaps your guitar is named Reggie and perhaps he lives in your study. Of course, he has a different home than your violin, Olivia—she lives in the downstairs family room. I believe animism is in our spiritual DNA. We feel the spirits and souls of these "things" and naturally treat them more appropriately as beings.

The animistic world is a nesting of souls within souls. There is the spirit of our earth, the spirit of continents and oceans, the spirit of the land on which we live, and all the spirits of the beings that live upon and within these places, whether they be man-made or nature made. For even the objects humans birth into being can be and are imbued with spirit. A birthing of a soul is a birthing of a soul. Anyone who is involved with creative projects will be well familiar.

Naming the Home

And so we arrive at the microcosm of our homes. The animist home where the spirits are recognized and everything lives somewhere. Perhaps you're doing the dishes and you're putting away your soup pot. Where does it go? Well, in the cabinet it lives in, of course. You also put away the leftovers from the big pot of soup you made into the fridge. Her name is Big Bertha. In fact, that really is the name of the fridge in our house. I named her so because it just came to me one day. I firmly believe the voice I heard was her telling me. She is the grandest refrigerator I've ever lived with. She's a reliable soul. Of course, Bertha lives in our house, which has its own spirit. A soul as important as the home one lives in deserves the honor of a name too, right?

In the United States, it would seem that naming one's home has fallen by the wayside, at least for a number of years now. My European friends are often telling me how much more commonplace it is to name homes, buildings, and estates large and small in Europe than it is in the States. You still see such wonderfully descriptive and soulful naming in small inns and bed and breakfasts. They serve as great examples, with names such as Orchard View Inn, Magnolia Cottage, or Sea Breeze Manor. Frankly, I think it's an animistic practice worth both maintaining and reviving! Our dwellings aren't strangers and ought not remain nameless. It doesn't matter whether you rent or own your home or whether it is large or small, nor does it matter the fanciness or humbleness. Our homes should function as our sacred sanctuaries. Of course, this makes arriving upon just the right name important.

Selecting and Declaring Your Home's Name

Naming your home is a good way to embrace your animistic beliefs. However, how do you begin going about finding your home's name? Well, it is a process that will take some consideration. The duration of this process will vary; however, you will know when you've arrived upon a proper name. You can begin observing the physical characteristics of your home's architecture and style. Is it a multi-floor home with a number of bedrooms and multiple bathrooms that feels well appointed with antiques you've collected? Perhaps it feels like a "manor." Is it a smaller house, with a quaint yard, and a cute little fence. A few pots of flowers on your doorstep? Perhaps the vibe you feel is "cottage." Maybe you live in studio apartment in the city that feels more like a "niche" or a "burrow"!

Look at the natural surroundings of your home, whether you live in the city or the country. Are you in a valley? Are you near the ocean? On the side of a mountain? Look at what types of plants and trees are in your yard, surround your home, and are prevalent throughout your neighborhood. Take notice what their characteristics are and how they grow: singularly or in groups, wild or landscaped. For example, do you have towering oaks, lone pines, bramble patches, birch stands, or vining ivy?

Next, examine the wildlife in your neighborhood. There is no room for anthropocentrism in my animism! Therefore, the wildlife should be considered equal and non-human neighbors. Do you see herds of deer? Are there turtles in the nearby stream? Perhaps there is a family of cottontail rabbits. Wait a minute—what's that familiar *caw* you hear? Ah yes, a trio of crows high up in that maple tree.

Now find a peaceful place to sit that makes sense to you to enter into meditation and listen to the spirit of your home. Perhaps this place is seated before the hearth. Perhaps it is on your front porch. It may even be under a tree on the property. Sit a moment with your eyes open and take several deep breaths. When you feel comfortable and calm in your location, close your eyes and continue to take a few deep breaths before resuming regular breathing. Simply listen with your sixth sense (also sometimes referred to as your inner senses). Let all the information you've just collected about your home swirl in your mind as it wishes. Allow yourself to connect with the spirit of your home. Trust what starts to form at the forefront of your mind. Ideas, words, and images will naturally float to the front of your mind. You will get a sense of what things might be right for potential names for your home. When you feel ready, open your eyes, take a moment to ground yourself, and write down some notes of your ideas in a journal.

You might even make a mind map or association web and see what combinations present themselves. Play with the permutations. It will likely be a combination of the different elements we discussed earlier. Perhaps you live in the country with a driveway that winds through a wooded patch to your small house. That could combine into Winding Wood Cottage. Perhaps your large suburban home has a big oak tree in the backyard and at night you hear the soft call of an owl. Perhaps you live at Owl-Oak Manor. Tiny apartment in a big city high-rise with an eastern view? Perhaps your abode may be called Sunrise Roost! Or perhaps your ancestral family crest has a lion on it and your family is into gardening and homesteading . . . you can call your home Lion's Den Farm. You get the idea!

Bringing the Name to Life

Once we've named our home, it's time to declare and use that name. How, you might ask? One of the first ways you might do so is to create a sign with its name. You can hang it outside your home or in an appropriate place indoors, like an entryway, a dining room where the family gathers, or perhaps your hearth. You can paint it, carve it, wood burn it, or create it in any method you see fit. You often see such placards on historic buildings, but why should the honor be relegated to those only? Gift your home with a placard of its name!

Another way, of course, is to simply use the name. Refer to your home by its name in conversations with friends. You'll be surprised how quickly they adopt using it to refer to your home as well! You'll even start to see friends who are "in the know" send you mail using it. So long as your name is on the envelope, the mail does find its way there. It's rather enchanting when you get mail to "Susie Smith, Berry Patch Bungalow, 123 Big Road." If you use your home's name, it won't take long to catch on!

It can be useful in magical workings as well, just as using a person's name is when you send healing to a person, for example. When you send protection or healing to a place, you can also use its name. If you have a hurricane barreling down toward a friend's home and want to send prayers for protection, you could then send it to the Deer Trod House in City, State. The more we discuss it, the more this type of animistic viewpoint toward our home likely makes sense. When everything that is is alive, it doesn't seem out of place to have a name for something like our home so that we may properly address that living being.

In a world alive with energy and the view that our relationship with living spirits should be reciprocal, it only makes sense that we honor our homes with offerings as well. You can pour blessed water offerings at the base of a special tree in your yard; you could burn a special house blessing incense periodically on your home's hearth, household altar, or mantle; or maybe you bless some birdseed to put into the feeder on your apartment's balcony. What should you offer your home? Ask it and listen—it will tell you.

As you can see, animism has never really left us, even for those who don't realize they are practicing it. Do you live in an animist home? Perhaps it's time to consciously embrace and acknowledge it and all the spirits abuzz around you. Perhaps you'll even be so moved to find your home's name! Next time you are lovingly greeted by your home after a long and difficult day, perhaps you can greet it in return, by name.

A Pocket Full of Change: Using Coins in Your Magick

Raechel Henderson

M oney, it is said, makes the world go round. While that can be debated on various fronts (from astronomical to metaphysical), it is true that capitalism and its accumulation of wealth before all else has an outsize impact on people's lives. Commerce is often treated as a taboo subject in magic circles. There are adages that one shouldn't perform spells for pay or read the tarot for cash. On the other hand, money is discussed as a type of energy by some in the occult, as a way to perhaps divorce it from the market. All of this makes talking about money and spellwork complicated. But just because it is difficult doesn't mean we shouldn't delve into the ways that money can be used in our magick.

Specifically, here, I'm looking at coins. Coins, I find, are really useful materia magica because they are portable and plentiful and tap into various energies—earth, wealth, metal, travel, prosperity, abundance, and so on. On their face, they can be used in jar spells, pouches, and talismans. But I want to dig a little deeper, looking at not only the iconography of various coins, but also their metal makeup and how that can be used to cast highly specialized spells. Because I am American, I am most familiar with the currency of the United States, and so that is the focus of my writing here. You can extrapolate from the ideas that follow, however, to work out ways to incorporate other coinage into your magick practice.

Coins minted in the United States are currently made up of zinc (for pennies) and cupronickel, a composition of copper and nickel (for nickels, dimes, and quarters). The metals do have their own magickal energies, and all of them have been used in various ratios in coins since the country started minting its own currency. Nickel has properties related to the home and opening doors (among others), which makes it a very useful metal for commerce magick. Copper conducts energy and has healing properties as well as energies associated with prosperity and change. Zinc is useful for warding and invisibility, which makes it a perfect metal to be used in the penny, a coin that some would like to see removed from circulation.

In the past, however, coins were minted from metals like silver, bronze, and even steel, which gives us even more flexibility in our spellcasting. To that point, I want to focus on three different coins: the wheat penny, the buffalo nickel, and the Mercury dime. These three coins were minted with higher amounts of costly metals than subsequent coins. They are also more likely to be found in circulation than previous versions that have even higher proportions of precious metals.

The Wheat Penny

The wheat penny is easily recognizable with the profile of Abraham Lincoln on one side and two heads of wheat on the other. Its composition has varied widely since it was originally minted, with a few notable years including metals one wouldn't expect to find in coins. For example, in 1909 and then again in the years 1946 to 1958 the Wheat Penny had tin in the mix, along with bronze, copper, and zinc. Tin, which has magickal properties related to knowledge and divination as well as softening, makes such pennies perfect for charm-casting oracles, as well as spells in which you are trying to soften someone's attitude or stance. If you are trying to influence someone to see things your way, you can carry this coin on you when interacting with them.

In 1943, the wheat penny was made from 100 percent steel and plated with zinc. The zinc would corrode, and the penny would turn silver-green. Steel shares the same magickal properties as nickel. With its zinc coating, this coin is well-suited for any spells in which you are trying to find a way into something through stealth or back channels. Add it to spell jars related to finances when you need to find previously unthought-of ways to make money. Or utilize it in protection spells when you want your home to be overlooked on physical, astral, and magickal planes.

Maybe you are looking to wage magickal war against corporations, billionaires, or capitalism itself. Or maybe you want to work to support and defend labor unions. The wheat penny minted between 1944 and 1946 would be a very valuable spell component. The bronze that coated the outer layer of these pennies was bronze made from spent shell casings. This was due to a metal shortage thanks to World War II. The energy of these pennies is aggressive and active. Bronze has magickal energies of communication and resilience, and this bronze in particular has an active and aggressive aura. These pennies are for spells that sound a clarion call for change. Wear them in pouches when participating in strikes and protests against exploitative corporations.

Bad Penny Hex

The Salvation Army is known for being trans- and homophobic, along with pushing an Evangelical Christian doctrine that is more interested in judging who is worthy of help than actually giving that help. Every holiday season, volunteers set up camp outside of shops, ring their bells, and collect donations. Usually I ignore them, but recently I decided to take a more magickal approach. I call it the Bad Penny Hex, and it involves taking pennies, usually the dingiest, most scuffed up ones I can find, and charging them with bad and negative energy. I visualize the penny giving off the most offensive, antagonistic aura, one that repels others, thus driving away people who would otherwise drop their loose change into the red buckets. I imagine the organization going bankrupt and having to dissolve. I spend time envisioning a holiday season free of their ringing bells. And then I drop those pennies into the buckets. It's the kind of hexing that coins were made for.

The Buffalo Nickel

Also known as the "Indian head" nickel, this coin features what is meant to represent a "Native American," a design drawn by a white man. The reverse depicts an American bison. The original coin, minted between the years of 1913 and 1938, are composed of 75 percent copper and 25 percent nickel. Due to its history, this coin is best used in spellwork regarding Indigenous and conservation/ecological issues. The generic profile, said to be an amalgamation created from the likenesses of several Indigenous tribe chieftains, focuses the energies on the many people of

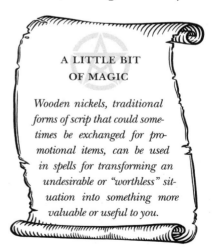

A LITTLE BIT OF MAGIC

Wooden nickels, traditional forms of scrip that could sometimes be exchanged for promotional items, can be used in spells for transforming an undesirable or "worthless" situation into something more valuable or useful to you.

the Americas who were and continue to be oppressed by white supremacy and the government.

Using the coin adds economic energies, leading one to naturally look at spells that target financial interests that are aligned against Indigenous peoples. Nickel's energies for opening doors paired with copper's properties of prosperity further refine the buffalo nickel's usefulness for spells aimed at fundraising. This can be taken even further by including the coin in freezing or binding spells to target the funds of corporations or organizations that are actively harming Indigenous populations.

The Mercury Dime

The Mercury dime, minted between 1916 and 1945, contains 90 percent silver and 10 percent copper. The head side depicts Liberty wearing a winged cap. The reverse shows a *fasces* and an olive branch. The fasces is a bundle of wood that is bound together and is a symbol of unity and strength. Fun fact—it has been a symbol of the National Fascist Party in Italy as well as being the word from which we get *fascism*. The olive branch symbolizes peace. The whole design is, symbolically speaking, a hot mess. Which might lead some to think that it isn't very useful as materia magica, no matter the silver content. I don't agree, however, because Witchcraft is an art built on subversion. Here we have a coin that seems tailor-made for some "Nazi Punks Fuck Off" magick.

The concept of liberty as a value and as a deity has been used in the past in politics. Combined with the fasces, this makes the Mercury dime perfect for spells targeting politicians, governments, officials, and political parties. With the links to fascism in not only the fasces but in the symbology of strength and unity, the political leanings of those this magick would work the best against is pretty clear, but I'll spell it out: any conservative, fascist, or authoritarian ideology that would sacrifice the individual to consolidate power.

While silver is good for protection on an energetic and psychic level, it also serves as an amplifier for and conductor of magickal energy. This means that it is going to enhance and broadcast not

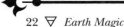

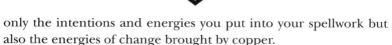

only the intentions and energies you put into your spellwork but also the energies of change brought by copper.

Wear or carry the Mercury dime when you are going to BLM and anti-fascist protests. Add it to any spellwork that targets groups that seek to gain strength and unity through the oppression of others. Draw out the energies of liberty and peace from the coin and use them to banish the authoritarian energies. Use the image of the fasces as your focal point, ascribe it to the group you are working against, and visualize it broken easily and permanently. Add the coin to your altar for any anti-fascist spellwork you are doing over a length of time. If you are sending money to groups such as the ACLU, the Anti-Defamation League, or Human Rights Watch, consecrate your donation by placing the coin on the check or cash donation or on the print-out of the receipt for your donation if it was made online. If you are collecting or working money magick to bring in donations for such organizations, make the Mercury dime the first piece of materia magica in your spell jar or other working.

A final note: despite bearing the image of Liberty, the coin is commonly called the Mercury dime due viewers to confusing the two. This adds another layer of significance to the dime, making it appropriate to use in spells for trans issues. It is especially effective to use in magick meant to protect trans people from harm by transphobic people and organizations. If you are making a protective pouch, talisman, or spell for yourself or a trans friend, this is a good coin to add. Before using the coin, hold it in your hands during the full moon and suffuse it with aggressive, protective energies. Any harm leveled at the person to be protected should be bounced back at the assailant in kind. Despite the olive branch on the reverse side, this is not a time for peace: if someone looks to break a trans woman's leg, they get the damage sent back to them. Witchcraft often uses the Bible for spellcasting. This is definitely "eye for an eye" territory.

Change for Change

Coins become symbols of the country that mints them. As such, they are powerful materia magica that can be used in spells targeting the government, corporations, and concepts like worker exploitation, living wages, and social justice issues. That coins travel around, passing through various hands, gives them momentum and energy that can be included in your spells. And their physical makeup gives you access to powerful energies. Search your couch cushions, dig through your change jar, or keep an eye out for a lucky penny on the street, and soon you'll have a handful of components for some powerful magick.

Obeah:
Afro-Caribbean Witchcraft

Emma Kathryn

The world is such a beautiful and mysterious place, and this is reflected in the many and varied spiritual and magickal traditions, paths, and practices found all over the world. Obeah is one such practice.

Obeah has its origins in West Africa but can be found throughout the Caribbean islands. While some of the traditions that come under the umbrella of African Traditional Religions (ATR) have become more widely known and accepted, obeah still remains something of a mystery.

So what exactly is obeah?

Magick and Spirituality

Obeah is a magickal and spiritual system that hails from West Africa. It was transported to the Caribbean islands by way of the slave trade when thousands of enslaved people were taken from Africa to work the sugar plantations. The enslaved had lost so much—their families, their homes, their freedom—so it is no wonder they clung to their beliefs. As people escaped the plantations, many helped by the indigenous peoples of the islands, their beliefs and practices mingled with those of the indigenous tribes. Because of this mixing of peoples and beliefs, today when we look at obeah within the Caribbean, we can see a beautifully diverse practice.

My family comes from Jamaica and so this is the form of obeah I practice, but even if you were to take ten practitioners from the same region of the same country, you would see ten different and unique practices! In part, this owes to the fact that there is no holy book or dogma within obeah, but it also highlights just how much of a personal practice obeah is and the power the obeah man or woman has in determining what their practice looks like.

In essence, obeah is a spirit work practice. In terms of practical magick, everything that occurs does so on many levels, including the spiritual. In this way, the obeah practitioner seeks to work at the spiritual level to resolve issues and problems or to effect the change they want to see in the world.

Many people often ask whether obeah is a closed practice, and in truth the answer depends on whom you ask. Some people believe obeah should only be practiced by those with links to the culture, while other practitioners are open to teaching others from outside of the culture. What is important, though, is that one requires a teacher to learn obeah. It isn't something that can be learned from books. A period of apprenticeship is needed before initiation onto the path can occur.

Deities and Spirits

While obeah practitioners, generally speaking, do believe in a supreme creator, it is regarded as being so far removed from humanity that it is completely unknowable to us. Instead, we work with spirits who intercede between us and it. These spirits include nature spirits, the spirits of the dead, and others still. In this way, obeah can be described as being animistic; indeed, the natural world is alive with spirit . . . there's nothing supernatural about magick because it is natural! With that said, there are some important obeah spirits, and it is useful for any aspiring initiate to learn more about them.

Sasabonsam

Sasabonsam is perhaps the most important spirit within obeah, for he is the one who gives *obi*, the power behind obeah. It is this transfer of power that can be described as a spirit initiation. In African and Caribbean folklore, Sasabonsam is often depicted as a monstrous being that lurks in the treetops in the deepest part of the forest, waiting to snatch up those who stray too far. The truth, though, is that he is a protective nature spirit who protects nature from those who may wish to destroy it for their own greed, though for the apprentice, this can still be daunting in the beginning. Sasabonsam invites us to overcome our fears so that we can become all

we can be, and as great as that sounds, it can be a hard process as we transcend the bounds of our comfort zones.

Papa Bones

Papa Bones is another important spirit within obeah. If Sasabonsam is the power within obeah, then Papa Bones is the guardian of that power. I often describe the relationship between Papa Bones and Sasabonsam as similar to that between a gardener and a garden. As the garden is nature itself, so is Sasabonsam the power, but it is the gardener who looks after and tends the garden, and so Papa Bones is the gatekeeper, the one who protects the power of obeah. While it may be Sasabonsam who initiates, it is Papa Bones who decides who may enter, who opens the way. It is said that Papa Bones has many different forms and functions, as many as there are bones in the human skeleton!

Asase

Asase is a female spirit and can be seen as the divine earth. Asase is also known as the Lady of the Pitch Lake or Kumama and represents the dual nature of the natural world. Nature is life giving and life affirming. Every living thing comes from nature, and nature creates the perfect breeding ground (pun not intended!) for life, from the warming sun to cool, refreshing water and all the resources that make life more comfortable. Nature is nurturing. And yet there is a destructive aspect to nature. Nature can be hard. The warming sun also burns; the cool, refreshing waters flood and drown; and droughts, hurricanes, and heavy snow can all be life threatening at their most extreme. And so in this way, Asase can often feel like a cold, aloof spirit. Not cruel but perhaps instead indifferent.

Anima Sola

Anima Sola is another female spirit. Though she is sometimes depicted as St. Bernadette, it would be a mistake to confuse and conflate Anima Sola with any other figure. *Anima sola* means "lonely soul." In Catholic mythology, she is a figure in purgatory, and she requires not only the help of God but also the help of the living. This hints at her role as an intermediary within obeah. She intercedes between the obeah practitioner and the other spirits. Anima Sola is a fiery spirit and can be intimidating to work with, as she requires that we see the world and everything in it as it is, including ourselves. She burns away the ego, revealing who we are at our core, and sometimes this can be difficult, as nobody is perfect. We all have those things we may not like about ourselves. The obeah practitioner is one who can reconcile the different parts of themselves and accept themselves and the experiences that have shaped them.

Making Magick

And so we get to that all-important question: What does an obeah practitioner do? Well, the answer depends on the person! I work with spirits to effect change. But this is the same answer I give when asked what I do in my Witchcraft practice, so is obeah a form of Witchcraft? I would say yes, or at least it is how I practice. I perform rituals and spellwork using herbs, plants, minerals, and so on. I work with spirit and the ancestors. I perform divination using cowrie shells. I often tell my students that many of the tools are the same no matter the tradition or path because, quite simply, they work. In this way, we can see many similarities between Witchcraft and many other magickal practices.

What makes obeah different besides the individual spirits is the training. We have already seen that obeah is a path involving initiation and that this initiation is one of spirit; however, it is important that the would-be obeah practitioner find someone to apprentice under. This period of tutelage is vital and involves building relationships with the different spirits as well as learning shell casting (a form of divination), rituals, and the tools of the trade. However, it can often be difficult to find an obeah practitioner to apprentice under.

So what does this mean for those who are interested in learning the craft? I often advise folks who are interested in obeah to start with developing an ancestor practice. Obeah is a spirit work practice and the ancestors are spirits, so it makes sense to start here—after all, everyone has ancestors. For many people, this working with the ancestors is often enough, but for some, it is the extra push they need to step more fully onto the path.

Crafting an Ancestor Spirit Bottle

An easy way to begin working with your ancestors is to set up a simple ancestor altar that can include pictures, candles, and mementos of your beloved dead. I also encourage people to make and use ancestor spirit bottles. These act as anchors that allow the ancestors to have a deeper connection here in the earthly realm, thus deepening the connection between you and them.

You will need:
Clean glass jar with a lid
Crushed eggshell (this represents life)
Sand or soil (representing the earthly realm)
Dried mugwort or dandelion (associated with spirit work)
Rosemary (for remembrance)
Items associated with the ancestor it is made for. This might be a
    memento, a favorite flower, or a piece of jewelry.
A white candle

Begin by layering the eggshell and sand in the jar until it is half full. Then add the other items. Put the lid on and seal it with wax from the candle. Now it's time to consecrate the jar for its particular purpose. If you already have a set practice, then create sacred space however you normally do. For beginners, it is enough to just clean the room you are in before lighting the candle. Spend as long as you need in meditation, and when you are ready, begin your call to your ancestor. I often advise people to begin with an ancestor they knew in life, as this is often an easier connection to make. To call to them, you can chant their name and lineage as far back as you can remember. For example, you might say something like this:

> *Blood of my blood, I call to you.*
> *Blood of my blood, I call to you.*
> *John Doe, son of Jane Doe and James Doe,*
> *I call to you.*
> *I invite you to reside in this vessel I have prepared for you.*
> *Blood of my blood, I call to you.*
> *Blood of my blood, I call to you.*

You can repeat this as a chant as many times as you feel is necessary. When you have finished, keep the vessel on your ancestor altar and use it whenever you wish to spend some time in devotion to them. This might be as simple as lighting a candle, calling to them, and leaving an offering.

Obeah can at times be a difficult path to follow, but sometimes the most challenging things are also the most worthwhile.

Talismans, Amulets, and Charms

Charlynn Walls

As practitioners of magic, we look for ways to enhance and increase the energy of our spellwork. We want to do so because it raises the probability of a successful spell. One way to increase the likelihood of an effective spell is to create talismans, amulets, and charms. Each of these items provides their own way to increase our magical energies and allows access to them over an extended time period. These items can also provide a tangible link to the spell, which helps us to later reinforce the magic when needed.

Charms

You may have already used charms in your magical practice without even realizing it. Typically, within our rituals and spells we will chant or create magical phrasing or words. That is the essence of a charm. They can be vocalized or written. Charms can also be used in conjunction with magical hand gestures or body movements to add even more emphasis and power to the spell. Charms are a great place to start because they can provide a building block for talismans and amulets and can be used in conjunction with both.

I have often utilized charms when composing a ritual. In order to raise the energy within a rite, we will often do so with the words that are repeated or chanted during the creation of the spell itself. It can also take written form, wherein you may write the words on paper or parchment. An example of this would be when you want to expand your own spiritual boundaries. In order to do so, you would write down an area you would like to experience growth in. This would occur during the main part of the ritual. Then the written charm could be kept as a reminder of your intention or burned as part of releasing your intention into the universe. During the rite, I've often chanted or said the words out loud as well. There are numerous ways you can include them in your practice.

One way that I've previously utilized a charm is during the casting of the Lesser Banishing Ritual of the Pentagram. In it, you utilize the words or sounds associated with each position/point of the pentagram. As you intone each, you also perform an action. Each movement and sound/word that is invoked is with a specific intention in order to remove negativity. I have found, along with my coven members, that it is highly effective in this regard. It provides consistent results, which would be expected given its intent, intonations of words/sounds, and symbolic gestures

Talismans

A talisman traditionally is an object that is imbued with magical properties that benefit the owner. Really any item could be utilized for this purpose, but those that are small enough to carry are most common because they are portable and can go with the individual using them. Talismans are created for specific magical purposes. In order to make one, you would want to look at the correspondences

for the time period when you would like to create your own talisman. In doing so, the talisman will be actively releasing the energy collected within during its creation to help you create the desired manifestation.

I have created talismans to actively provide protection for myself and others. The design, color, and other correspondences were active considerations in my spellwork. I would often revisit these when recharging the object. For instance, there was a time when I was concerned that someone was actively performing hexes against myself and members of my coven. I wanted to help cut off their attack, so I created a talisman. Since it was a talisman for protection, I used a black object, in this case a rock I had a connection with, a piece of obsidian in the shape of a magic mirror. I had studied geology for a long time and had an affinity for rocks and minerals. The shape helped me see the magic being reflected to the caster.

In order to continue to utilize the protection originally produced in the initial spell, I needed to recharge it during the waning moon in order to banish negative intentions. It actively helped me in my protection magic by allowing me to gradually release the magic contained during the creation of the spell. This allowed me to continue carrying it until I felt the issue had been neutralized.

Amulets

Amulets are usually associated with luck and are often referred to as good luck charms. These are objects that protect one from trouble, ill health, or bad luck. Amulets are more general in their application. These items can be either naturally occurring or created.

I was of course most familiar with the four-leaf clover, the rabbit's foot, and the horseshoe that is hung with the ends pointing upward. These are passive objects that are utilized in order to produce a desired effect. While it is not uncommon for these items to be held or carried by the practitioner, amulets are most often worn. One amulet that I often wore in my early days as a magical practitioner was that of the rune *Algiz* ᛉ, which wards off evil. Since I was not sure if there were any active workings against me, this was passive work to ensure that no negativity or evil was to come near me. It was also beneficial to my peace of mind as a new practitioner of the Craft.

Combining All Three: A Healing Ritual

The following is a healing ritual that will utilize a talisman, an amulet, and a charm in order to maximize the energy within each item. By doing, so we will capitalize on our intention, connection, and energetic vibrations to produce the best possible results. This will be a formal ritual that should be conducted on a Wednesday, which is associated with Hermes and Mercury and therefore healing. It could also be completed during a New or Waxing Moon, which would allow for the practitioner to harness the power of regeneration. The following ritual can be shortened as appropriate for whatever you want to accomplish.

To begin, set up your altar area. Place four quarter candles in their corresponding directions. For a healing ritual, you may want to include green or white candles in order to take advantage of their vibrational energies. Prepare a small bowl of salt water to help you cleanse your talisman and amulet. A talisman I recommend for healing is a small rod of Asclepius, which represents the Greek god of healing. You could purchase one or create it out of a sculpting clay.

For the amulet, I would personally choose a bloodstone to represent the body (the red of the stone to represent the blood) and the desired outcome (green to represent the healing). Of course, pick symbols and stones that have meaning to you. Other items that you could include on the altar to aid in your work for healing are aventurine, thyme, willow bark, and apple. You will also need a small pouch to hold the amulet and charm.

Be sure to bless the salt water before beginning. Hold your hands over the water and close your eyes. Feel the energy build up through your core and feel yourself pushing it into the liquid. As you push the energy into the water, say the following charm three times:

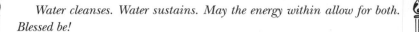

Water cleanses. Water sustains. May the energy within allow for both. Blessed be!

Cast your circle by calling the quarters. As you move to each one, dip your fingers into the water and sprinkle it while calling the quarters.

Calling the Quarters

North: I call to the powers of the north, the guardians of the earth. Bless us by allowing us to feel the earth and its stabilizing influence. We welcome you to our circle!

East: I call to the powers of the east, the guardians of air. Bless us with the breath of life. We welcome you to our circle!

South: I call to the powers of the south, the guardians of fire. Bless us with the heat that allows us to purge the unnecessary. We welcome you to our circle!

West: I call to the powers of the west, the guardians of water. Bless us with the restorative waters to that give life. We welcome you to our circle!

Invocation

Set out the items you will be working with within easy reach. Place the talisman and amulet in the remaining saltwater in order to begin cleansing them. At this time, you may want to sit and contemplate the healing you are working for in depth. What are you healing or working to heal?

Take the parchment from your altar and set it in front of you to inscribe your charm on it. Write on the parchment, "Water cleanses. Water sustains." As you are writing, focus on the intent of the words, which is to remove the illness or what is keeping the individual unwell and working to provide a sustained change in them. Keep this written charm to include with your amulet.

At this point, take the rod of Asclepius or your chosen object to be your talisman and work with it to imbue it with magical intent and energy. This object will be the one that is actively working to

manifest your intent and will be gradually releasing the energy until you renew it again. You will chant the charm that you initially wrote out as you hold your talisman. Say the chant over and over to increase the energy in your ritual. As you say the words out loud, feel the energy being created and push it out from yourself and into the talisman. As you feel the energy begin to swell in the circle, let it burst forth. The energy not stored in the talisman will flow out into the universe in order to help you manifest your will.

Take the bloodstone, or your chosen amulet, that was cleansed earlier and place it with the written charm into the pouch. This amulet can be carried with you or with the person the healing work is being done for. It will work to keep any further damage or injury from occurring.

Cakes and Ale

During this time, take a moment to recharge. Eat a bit of cracker or cake and drink something. Using the opportunity to bring yourself into balance emotionally, spiritually, and physically will allow you to support your work for healing. Also, take this chance to note anything unusual or interesting that transpired during the ritual. You may want to reflect on it later.

Releasing the Quarters

West: Powers of the west, I thank you for your time and your restorative and healing properties. Hail and farewell!

South: Powers of the south, I thank you for your time and your gentle heat that allowed us to purge the unwelcome. Hail and farewell!

East: Powers of the east, I thank you for your time and your gentle winds that eased our breathing. Hail and farewell!

North: Powers of the north, I thank you for your time and your strength that kept me strong and stable. Hail and farewell!

Closing the Circle

Take a moment to contemplate the rite and clearly envision all that you have worked for. Take time to again thank all entities who gathered with you at this time. End by saying,

The circle is now open but unbroken. Hail and farewell!

As with any other magical working, make sure to support this rite through practical applications. In this instance you could make sure that you are getting the proper amount of sleep and nutrition for proper functioning. Also, support your work by following your doctor's directives. If they said to take medication for a condition or issue, do so! Doing all parts, both mundane and magical, will ensure the best outcome.

Conclusion

When utilizing a talisman, amulet, charm or any combination of those items, you should know what your need is. Once you know what you need, you will be able to address your intention and create a ritual, rite, or spell to produce the desired result. Always utilize these in conjunction with practical applications in order to maximize the effectiveness of the energies being utilized. This may mean supporting the magic with diet and exercise if you are working for healing or health.

It helps when you have a connection to the talisman, amulet, or charm that you are creating. Finding what works for others is a good jumping-off point, but you want to make sure that you can identify and connect with the symbols or wording used. Always use what works best for you, as it will increase the probability of your spell coming to fruition. Find the item that connects you to your spiritual work and tap into it, creating the perfect complement to your spiritual work.

Air Magic

Whisk In the Magick with Your Own Besom and Purifying Wand

JD Walker

Other than a cauldron, is there any tool in a Witch's trade more iconic than a besom? Probably not. The same can be said of the purifying wand. Both tools are used for cleansing a person or area prior to ritual or magickal workings.

History

Besoms have been in use since humans settled down (even temporarily) in one spot. Something had to be used to clear away the limbs and twigs before hunkering down before the campfire. After people moved into caves and later huts, the besom was needed to brush the ashes from around the fireplace or sweep the critters, bugs, and children outdoors. The term *besom* originally meant a stick with twigs or foliage tied around it. The word *broom* came into prominence when our British ancestors began to prefer a besom made from *Genista,* or broom plant.

The original besom was probably a branch from a nearby shrub. It didn't last too long but could do the job well enough. After some time, somebody thought of making a thicker broom by lashing several short branches or bundles of grass or twigs to a sturdy stem with leather thongs or plaited rope. This lasted a little longer.

It wasn't until the eighteenth century that brooms as we know them started to show up. Flat, manufactured brooms came a little later still. They had the advantage of lasting much longer than the bundle of twigs on a stick.

Tools for smoke cleansing used to mean a simple feather and a smoldering bit of incense in a pot or on a plate. In time, worshippers and religious leaders developed very ornate pots on chains that were filled with charcoal and herbs and swung ceremoniously through the ritual space or through a gathering of the flock by a designated thurifer (religious acolyte).

We have North American Native populations to thank for the most common tool for smoke cleansing today: the bundle of leaves and stems from the white sage plant (*Salvia apiana*). While Native Americans may have used white sage predominately, today's practitioners will likely find sage bundles blended with any number of added herbs, such as lavender, cedar, rosemary, eucalyptus, and more.

Using sage bundles in ritual or for general cleansing is a perfectly good practice. However, some people worry about the stigma of cultural appropriation when using this very sacred Native American practice. Others express concern about the overuse of *S. apiana* and the possible impact on the environment from less than mindful harvesting of a native desert plant.

Fortunately, "smoke cleansing" doesn't have to mean "saging." Cultures all around the globe have used a variety of herbs and resins to perform the task of cleansing with smoke. That brings us back to the burning bit of incense on a plate and the question of how to waft the smoke over the person, object, or place you are working with. As mentioned earlier, feathers are handy for this task. But you can also make a miniature broom or purifying tool to push the cleansing smoke in the direction you desire.

By the way, this same tool is also handy for asperging, or sprinkling scented and blessed water during ritual work.

A LITTLE BIT OF MAGIC

Perhaps the first depiction of women astride a broom comes in a fifteenth-century manuscript by Martin le Franc in his poem Le champion des dames, *a rare defense and celebration of women for the time period.*

Aspergers, or aspergillum, come to us from Jewish traditions. The first mention of them is made in the Jewish Torah and Christian Bible in Leviticus when a holy man cures a leper by sprinkling him with a tool made with a cedar stick, some hyssops, and a couple of birds. In a bit of grizzly history, one bird is killed and bled. The second is attached live to the cedar stick along with the herbs and the leper is sprinkled in blood.

Fortunately, the practice evolved to become based on sprinkling scented and blessed water on the afflicted, much to their relief, I'm sure. The tool evolved too. In Catholic churches where the practice continues, the priest is more likely to use a perforated metal ball on a handle to distribute the holy water on his flock.

Today's Uses

Today's Pagans make use of both of these tools. The besom or broom doesn't literally sweep the ground anymore. It is an air tool used to symbolically sweep away any negativity before casting a circle or preforming a magickal working.

The purifying wand is also an air tool, although it can be used as a water tool. Those who are participating in ritual or magickal work are often smoke cleansed with incense as well as being sprinkled with a scented or magickally blessed water.

The question often arises, do you really need a broom or a purifying tool to conduct your work? Technically, no. You can move around a ritual space using your arms to direct positive energy to push out any negativity. You can use your hand to wave incense smoke in the direction you desire.

However, having the right tools doesn't hurt. As with much of what we do, using the right tools in a properly constructed ritual space while dressed appropriately and mentally prepared for the project ahead can help to focus our intentions even stronger. It's like the difference between grabbing a meal at a fast food place and sitting down to a well-prepared meal laid out on the dining table. Both will satisfy your hunger. Only one will also satisfy your soul.

Making a Purifying Wand

For simplicity, let's start with a wand. Practically any plant material can be used to make a purifying wand. I frequently use pine or juniper. However, I have also gathered material from boxwoods, rosemary plants, Johnson grass, cleyera, and more. I do find that plants with smaller leaves or strap-like foliage make the best tools.

If your magickal working is specific, you might want to pair your choice of material to the purpose at hand. The foliage of junipers is healing and uplifting. Gather it to guard against accidents and illness. Yew or boxwood would make a perfect material to use to smoke cleanse yourself and your space during workings involving chthonic deities. Small-leafed Japanese holly twigs would be good to use for protective rituals.

To make the wand, you will need a stick about twelve inches long and about as thick as your forefinger. This can be a dowel stick from the local hardware store, or you can harvest a piece of oak, maple, pine or ash—whatever happens to grow in your area. You will also need some plant stems with roughly six inches of foliage. Three to four should make a reasonably full wand.

A tool of this size can be constructed using a heavy yarn or garden twine. Simply start by securely tying one of the stems to the bottom of the stick about three inches up from the base. Once it is firmly attached, add another stem to the left of the first and tightly wrap the twine around both stems. Continue adding stems, firmly wrapping each one as you go, until the tool is as full as you would like.

Tie the yarn in a double knot. To make your wand a bit more decorative, you can continue wrapping the yarn or twine around until you have a two-to-three-inch collar around the top of the stems. Tie the yarn off and tuck the knot under the last two circles of yarn.

This is a quick, temporary tool that will serve you well for several rituals or workings. You can make it as fancy as you like by

wrapping the handle in colored ribbons that coordinate with the seasons or the purpose of your working.

Once you've mastered the technique of wrapping a wand, it's just a matter of thinking bigger to make a besom.

Making a Besom

You are probably accustomed to seeing brooms made of straw. Technically, this is a type of sorghum (*S. bicolor*, syn. *Sorghum vulgare* var. *technicum*), specifically the tasseled tops of the sorghum. The flat, spread-out head of the straw broom wasn't invented until around the 1830s. Because this type of broom did a better job of gathering up dirt and debris, it quickly left the old besom in the dustbin.

You can quite literally grow your own broom using traditional broom corn, or broom straw.

Sorghum is a grass in the same family of plants as the sweet corn you may grow or purchase from the local farmers market. The difference is broom corn makes seed heads, not ears. If you can grow corn in your area, you can grow sorghum.

Like its corn cousin, sorghum needs to be planted in a loose, fertile soil in full sun that will get plenty of moisture while it is sprouting. Sorghum tolerates high heat and low moisture once it is established.

Plant broom straw after the last frost. Germination rates are low. That means you may have to place more seed in a row to insure a sufficient crop for your broom or wand. You can always thin out extra plants if they seem a little crowded after the seeds sprout.

Broom straw matures in about 120 days. When the sorghum begins to tassel, or form a head, farmers who do this for a living will bend the stalks over at about waist high in a practice that is called tabling. This forces the seed head to droop, but that's better than having it fan out and dry in a spraddled out fashion, as my grandmother would say.

Once it has reached maturity, the stalks are cut and hung upside-down to dry in a well ventilated area for two to three weeks.

The seeds are combed off, leaving the bare stems that will become the head of a broom or wand. From this point, you will be working with the material in the same manner as if you had gathered plant stems from the landscape.

Find a stick roughly four to six feet long and at least one inch in diameter. This will be your handle.

Because this will be a heavier tool, you will need something stronger than yarn to tie the plant stems to the handle. Leather strapping is ideal. You can use a very sturdy garden twine as well. In a pinch, clothesline rope will also work. In the broom industry, wire is used, and this will work fine for our purposes as well.

The material you cut for the head of your besom, whether straw or landscape stems, should be twelve to eighteen inches in length. Follow the instructions given for the wand for tying the stems to the handle. In this case, I recommend tying one circle of stems to the bottom six inches of the handle. Then, move up another six inches and tie another circle of stems to the handle. This will make for a nice, full besom. Just like the purifying wand, you can finish the besom by creating a collar on the upper six inches, wrapping the entire top of the stems with your leather strapping or twine to give the tool a finished look.

Dedicating Your Tools

Prepare your ritual space according to your tradition. Have your new tools on the altar. After calling the appropriate deities or guardians, take up the first tool. Cleanse it in the smoke of a purifying incense such as frankincense, sage, or copal. Next, purify it with blessed water or water that has cleansing essential oils mixed in. Ask your patron deity or guardian to bless and empower your new tool as well. Do the same with the second tool.

After ritual, store your tools as respectfully as you would your cauldron, Book of Shadows, or ritual clothing. They should only be used for magickal or spiritual work.

With proper care, your besom and purifying wand should serve you well for multiple rituals throughout the Wheel of the Year.

City Magic and Crossroads Spells

Sasha Graham

Witch! Say it out loud. Potent word, isn't it? The word *witch* packs a power punch whether personally embodied or screamed as an accusation. One of two images usually springs to mind when someone hears *witch*: the classic Halloween trope or a Pagan nature goddess. The image of a hag snug on her broom, with black cat and cone hat jetting across a fat Full Moon is enduring. The other side of the spectum offers up a hippie, earth goddess Witch, flower crown in place, weaving fairy enchantments, bathing in morning dew, and worshipping willow trees.

The Witch is placed in a natural environment under both assumptions. The classic Disney witch lives in a castle high in the mountains or thatched hut in the woods, far from civilization. A modern Witch is imagined in pastoral glory, in the herb gardens cultivating fresh botanicals and performing New Moon rituals in the darkest of nights.

The Witch's nature-magic connection makes sense. The Craft rightly posits that we are part of nature, not separate from it. Natural energies help us access inner power. Working in tandem with the Moon, Sun, and seasons fosters alignment for spell and ritual work. We court spirit allies, animals, and plant medicine to learn and grow. They share their wisdom with us. We share our energy with them. This is the alchemy of symbolic, imaginative, and psychological attuning. It is what makes our magic potent.

But magic is not exclusive to deep forests, sandy beaches, and strictly natural environments. Magic interconnects the entire universe. It exists everywhere. Thus, magic also thrives in urban environments, yet it is often overlooked there. Looking to connect with dynamic magic? Gaze no further than the nearest city.

Cities have unique seasonal rhythms. New York springs to life in the fall, Prague shimmers under winter snow, and Paris glimmers like

a jewel through spring rains. You can wrap a city's energy around you like a cloak. Use it to power your spells and rituals.

Urban areas contain treasure troves of powerful energy just waiting to be called upon when seeking to manifest something. Cities are often built upon trade routes and waterways holding their own unique power and mystique. Consider the energizing San Francisco Bay and the mysterious energy reverberating between Santa Barbara and the Channel Islands. It is no accident that enigmatic New Orleans became a zeitgeist of food, culture, and history right where the Mississippi River melts into the Gulf of Mexico. Cities are centers of commerce, creativity, and action. Talk about going straight to the power center!

Crossroads Magic

What makes cities especially powerful? Crossroads. Most cities are chock full of them! Crossroads are energetic conduits and potent locations for effective spellcasting. Manhattan is a tiny thirteen-mile island but packs a whopping 3,360 intersections. Is it an accident that Gotham is a center of international culture, art, finance, and media? Nope. It brims with intense energy, which can be harnessed when spinning a spell.

Crossroads are mysterious and rooted in ancient magic. They mark the space where clear conduits of energy intersect. Symbolically, a crossroads marks the intersection of the visible and invisible worlds. These liminal places mark the threshold between past and future. It is the in-between space of what once was and will soon be. Destiny rests in the personal choice you make when roads converge. Your road is your chosen path. Will you continue forward or adjust course when two paths cross and a new option presents itself?

A three-way crossroads is traditionally feminine, while a four-way crossroads is masculine. This association aligns with the numerical values of the Empress and Emperor of the tarot deck. The Empress is numbered three, marking creativity, while the Emperor is numbered four and reflects structure. Spirits, or the genii locorum, residing at crossroads are known as "gatekeepers" or "road openers." Curry their favor by leaving offerings and gifts such as foods, herbs, or precious stones.

Crossroads are historically packed with lore surrounding the place where two alternate realities meet. Crossroads were dangerous places before the advent of technology. There was no GPS to help you out after going two hours in the wrong direction after one wrong turn on your horse and buggy. Bandits and thieves often stalked crossroads and bridges as places where unsuspecting travelers could be caught off guard.

Ancient cultures placed powerful goddesses like the Greek goddess Hecate in the charge of a crossroad. Hecate was imagined with three faces aligning with the phases of the Moon and the Triple

Goddess: Maiden, Mother, and Crone. Hecate possesses the ability to see three converging roads at once. She possesses the wisdom of hindsight, insight, and foresight. Hecate understands all your possible outcomes. Her flickering torch provides guidance for souls seeking the entrance to the underworld. Death is a crossroads space between the physical world of life and the invisible potentials of what is to come. Curry Hecate's favor for protection and safety.

Monotheistic and masculine "anti-Pagan" cultures turned the magical essence of a crossroad into a dangerous and unholy thing. Traitors were hung at crossroads as warning to those who passed by. Anyone caught lingering at a crossroad could be accused of Witchcraft, tried, and executed. The devil replaced Hecate as one who lingers at the crossroads. Hecate's protection was replaced with a monstrous demon who will tempt you to sell your soul for all eternity.

Humans and spirits alike move through crossroads and leave traces of themselves behind. Times Square is called the "Crossroads of the World" because everyone who lives and visits New York City goes there to people watch, celebrate, and explore. Stand at 42nd Street and 7th Avenue to stand in the footsteps of past and future presidents, celebrities, and heads of state. Go there to commune with the energy of everyone from Marilyn Monroe to Jennifer Lopez, from Theodore Roosevelt to Winston Churchill, from the Beatles to BTS. They've all passed through and left traces of themselves behind.

Crossroads Spells

Crossroads are useful for casting spells and dissipating energy. For instance, you can leave a magical letter of intention or petition at the crossroads. Alternately, you can ensure responsible magical cleanup by depositing leftovers from a spell at a crossroads. Candle stubs, salt, water, cracked eggshells, or any spell remnants can be tidied up by dispersing them into the air, burying them, or placing them in a crossroads trash receptacle.

Take your crossroads magic one step further by utilizing a particular neighborhood's energy. Cast for style and glamour in the

fashion district. Cast for future travel at transportation hubs. Cast for power near government centers. Cast for peace and serenity near landscaped nature centers, parks, and fountains. Note the name of the roads passing through the crossroad. Can you use them to align with the energy of your desire? Imagine casting a spell for finance on Wall Street or a spell for fame and fortune on Hollywood Boulevard. Note the magical use of numbered streets. Cast stability and structure spells on a 4th Street intersection or a new beginning spell on a 1st Avenue.

Financial District Spell for Fiscal Flow

Perform this spell when looking for a financial windfall, to increase your bank account balance, spending power, and earning potential.

You will need:
Water
½ cucumber
Fresh mint leaves
4 shiny quarters
4-way crossroads in a financial district (or near a bank)

Financial centers tend to be full of a specific energy. Brooks Brothers suits and shiny polished shoes, power players and deal brokers. Let their energy fill you while casting this finance spell.

Prepare a drinkable infusion by filling up ¾ of a glass with water. Slice the green skin off of the cucumber. As you peel it away, imagine any negative financial fear or bad habit being discarded. Slice thin circles of cucumber, imagining they are coins. Imagine depositing money in the bank as you place them in the water. Cover with ice and set to chill in the fridge for 45 minutes. Imagine money growing. Ruminate on all the ways you will spend, save, and share your money. Remove the infusion after 45 minutes, add fresh mint leaves, and drink.

Take 4 quarters to the crossroads of the main financial district. Beginning in the east corner and working your way clockwise to the

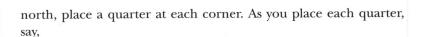

north, place a quarter at each corner. As you place each quarter, say,

> *Money, money, come to me.*
> *I am where you want to be.*

When you place your last quarter, turn to the north and walk into a future of financial abundance and pleasure.

Midnight Crossing Spell

Feeling stressed by a decision you must make? Reached a life transition and aren't sure which way to proceed? A door is opening. This simple spell will help you move through it effortlessly. Sunrise and sunset are liminal moments when night greets day and day dissolves into night. Solstices and equinoxes are the nether region where one season bleeds into the next. Midnight is the moment

when one day turns into another, and that's what makes this spell particularly powerful.

Select a three- or four-way crossroads in a neighborhood containing the energy you want to align with. Seeking beauty or inspiration? Go to the arts district. Seeking stability? Go to an upscale neighborhood. Looking to start your own company? Go to the business district.

Make your way to the crossroads so you arrive by at least 11:50 p.m. Linger while letting go of any stress or bad juju. Allow the delicious energy of possibility to accumulate. Imagine the very best-case scenario, and when midnight strikes, cross the road and move effortlessly into the future you desire.

Crossroads Spell to End to a Relationship

We all face moments when we must end a relationship or patterns of behavior. Performing this spell will aid you in your healing journey. The spell harms none when performed with a peaceful heart. It is a gentle way to snip the energetic cord between you and another person or behavior.

You will need:
Warm tea
Candle
Pen
Paper
Dried rose petals (Get in the habit of drying out old flowers for spells once they begin to fade!)
4-way crossroads with a traffic light or 4 stop signs

Set aside at least 30 minutes when you will not be disturbed. Brew a cup of your favorite tea and light a single candle. As you light the candle, focus on the flame and imagine yourself shining independently. Take the pen and paper and write a goodbye letter to the person or thing. Record any unspoken words or sentiments, gratitude for having known them, or why parting ways is the best way for you to practice self-care.

Bring the letter and a pocket full of dried rose petals to a four-way crossroads with a traffic light or four stop signs. Use a GPS to approach the crossroads from the south and moving north. This aligns with moving toward your highest truth. Imagine the person or thing moving beside you. As you reach the corner, imagine saying goodbye to them. Focus on the stop sign or wait for the light to turn red. Focus on the color red. See, hear, or say the word *stop*. In your mind's eye, watch them turn left and walk away into the night.

Continue forward and safely cross the street in the northern direction you were already moving. Deposit the unaddressed letter at the corner. Focus once again on the stop sign or red light. See, hear, or say the word *stop*. Gather a handful of rose petals and sprinkle them behind you as you walk away from the crossroads, continuing due north and saying,

That is over; now it's done.
What once was tethered's now unspun.
Moving forward, free at last.
Release my connection to the past.

The Witches' Alphabet

Kate Freuler

If you've been spending time in the Witchcraft world, there's a very good chance you're familiar with a set of symbols called the Theban alphabet. This collection of swirly, mysterious letters is sometimes referred to as the "Witches' alphabet" and is integrated into magical workings or used as a code in journals or spellbooks. It combines magic with secrecy; it can act as a cipher to disguise private information or add extra power to rituals that involve the written word.

The Theban script can be found online and in many books with a chart showing its correspondence to the modern English alphabet, which clearly displays that it can be used in place of common letters. However, finding deeper information about it can be a bit of a challenge. When I first stumbled across it many years ago, I wondered where and when this collection of symbols originated and how it came to be named the Witches' alphabet. Was it invented by modern Witches, or was it older than that?

It turns out that the reason it's so hard to find the exact story behind the Theban script is that there is very little historically factual information about it. Occultists have theorized for many years about its origins and uses, but ultimately there isn't one definitive answer. There are, however, various ideas that, when combined, paint a blurry picture of this ancient alphabet's past.

A History of Angels, Witches, and Scholars

The Theban alphabet was first published in the 1500s in a book by occultist Johannes Trithemius called *Steganographia*. In this book, the author accredited the symbols to Honorius of Thebes, a magus (magician or sorcerer) from the thirteenth century. It is said that Honorius of Thebes penned one of the oldest known grimoires in the world, *The Sworn Book of Honorius*. However, it's unclear whether this magus was a real person or simply a legend.

The myth of Honorius goes like this: At the time of the grimoire's creation, religious leaders were executing magicians and destroying ancient magical texts. Honorius was one of several magi chosen from various countries in Europe to transcribe existing sacred magical information into code to preserve and protect it. It's said he was elected by 811 master magicians to record seven volumes on the magical arts, which were dictated to him by angelic influences. The knowledge contained within Honorius's work was considered hallowed and top secret, to be seen only by those within the specified counsel of the magi. The books were not to be handled or possessed by anyone outside of this small sect and were occasionally destroyed upon the death of the owner if no suitable successor was available to inherit it.

The Theban alphabet is sometimes called Honorian alphabet after its supposed creator. References to the Theban alphabet can be found in some noteworthy tomes, including work by Heinrich Cornelius Agrippa; Dr. John Dee, who was the advisor for Queen Elizabeth I; and even Nostradamus. Over the centuries, occultist scholars developed various theories about the purpose of the cipher. Some surmised that it was given to humans by angels as a tool for defeating evil. Some claimed the script was invented simply to disguise magical information, protecting its practitioners from persecution during the witch hunts and similar inquisitions. The symbols vaguely resemble zodiac signs and, therefore, parallels were drawn to celestial significance. Some scholars ascribed elements, animals, and spirits to each of the letters. One thing that's certain is the letters correspond loosely to the Hebrew and Latin alphabets, opening the door to many possibilities about its use as a code.

In the 1950s, Gerald Gardner, known as the "Father of Wicca," played a large role in reigniting interest in the Theban alphabet among the growing magical community of the time. In his studies, Gardner delved deeply into various ancient scripts, including the Theban alphabet. He expanded further upon its meaning, demonstrating various practical ways to utilize it in modern magi-

cal applications. From this, the Theban script became accessible to the magical community in general. Since some Wiccans and other magical practitioners call themselves Witches, the Theban alphabet came to be known as the Witches' alphabet.

Mystery Is Power

Whether the Theban alphabet was created by angels, a community of magicians, or a mythical magus, nowadays it is used in many different ways by Witches, Pagans, and magical-minded people.

Like anything that is given mystical associations by many people over time, the script has gained power from the collective belief in its magic. Think about some common symbols that evoke strong emotions, such as the pentagram or cross. Technically, they are merely shapes; what gives them power is the widespread belief in their significance. This can be applied to the Theban alphabet too.

While its origins may seem wishy-washy, the script has been utilized by occultists, magicians, Witches, and other magically inclined people for hundreds of years. This means that its power has gained momentum in the collective unconscious, growing as people come to incorporate it into their practice and believe in its magical energy.

One might wonder, if the origins of this alphabet are so unclear and we don't know the true reason for its creation, why include it in magic? Understandably, some people prefer to stay away from symbols or materials that they don't fully comprehend. Others feel that it's the mystery itself that lends power to a spell or ritual. Including an enigmatic alphabet in your practice creates the sense that you're in touch with something ancient and powerful. This is further fueled by the understanding that the alphabet has enchanted magical practitioners for hundreds of years. Bringing the element of the unknown into a spell or ritual increases the belief that it will be successful. Additionally, there's no denying the power of visual impact, and the appearance of the Theban alphabet certainly adds a mysterious, esoteric look to any magical craft. While aesthetics aren't important to everyone, some people find that the appearance of their workings impacts their outcome.

Using the Witches' Alphabet

How to use the Witches' alphabet in your practice is limited only by your imagination, but at its core, there are two basic reasons to include it.

First, it is a cipher, meaning it's used to keep information secret. Some people prefer to write their Book of Shadows in code to keep the material hidden. Also, if someone is doing a ritual or spell in a space where others might see it, writing in an alternative alphabet will protect the working from unwanted influences or outsiders casting doubt at their goals.

Second, as mentioned, there is great power in that which is mysterious. Believing that the letters or symbols you incorporate into a spell have mystical undertones grants your working even more clout. Belief in the magic of the Theban alphabet is powerful psychologically, which strengthens the energy that goes into a working. When an object, ingredient, or symbol is loaded with significance or considered special in some way, it increases the belief that it will help manifest a desired outcome. That's why so many spells include tools imbued with meaning, such as a special herb dug up at midnight under a New Moon or a nail from an antique coffin. The

Theban script is no different and has accumulated energy and significance over centuries:

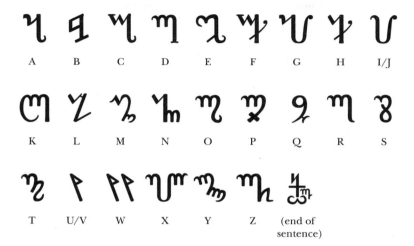

| A | B | C | D | E | F | G | H | I/J |

| K | L | M | N | O | P | Q | R | S |

| T | U/V | W | X | Y | Z | (end of sentence) |

As you can see, each symbol correlates to a letter. Many simple spells involve writing something on paper or wood, carving a name or phrase into a candle, or even an affirmation jotted on a sticky note and stuck to the bathroom mirror. Any of these simple examples of magical writing can be done with the Witches' alphabet, giving them an extra layer of power. While some practitioners who are extremely advanced in their studies of esoteric alphabets might use them for divination and other applications, generally the Theban script is used to simply transcribe writing from a common alphabet into a mystical one.

Spell for Personal Magical Power

This spell acts as a means of attracting magical power and confidence. This spell is appropriate to do when you're learning new things about Witchcraft or magic, when you're feeling low on magical energy and have hit a plateau in your practice, or you're finding that your rituals and spells just aren't working out as planned.

This working involves writing your own name in the Witches' alphabet. Seeing your personal moniker in an esoteric cipher achieves two things. It acts as a reminder of your innate magical power, while simultaneously drawing upon the cumulative mystical energy that has grown around the Theban script over the years. The name you choose should be the one you identify most closely with, particularly in terms of your magical life. This might not be your given name, but a nickname, screen name, or even a secret name you have for yourself.

You will need:
- Purple pen or pencil
- Piece of paper large enough to write your name on
- Tape
- Frankincense resin
- Charcoal disk for burning (You can replace the frankincense and charcoal disk with stick incense if you wish.)

This spell should be done at night on the Full Moon and can be performed inside or outside depending on your preference. Gather your materials in a time and place where you won't be disturbed.

Ignite the charcoal disk and place the frankincense on it to burn, or light your stick incense. Use the purple pen to write your name on the paper in the Witches' alphabet, based on the key provided on page 61. When you're done, spend a moment gazing at the symbols. Consider how magical your name looks now. These symbols, steeped in mystery and lore, connect the personal energy in your name to that of centuries of magicians who have also gazed upon them with wonder. Hold the paper in the smoke of the frankincense, imagining that it's imbuing your name with knowledge and inspiration.

When you feel the spell is complete, tape the paper with your name somewhere that you will see it every day, such as on a mirror you use to get ready each day or on your altar. Every time you see it, you'll be reminded of your power as a Witch or magical practitioner, while the symbols attract wisdom and inspiration into your magical life. This will help you gain confidence in your studies, strengthen your belief in your personal power, and bring a fresh spark into your practice.

You can tweak this spell by replacing your name with an empowering phrase or a clearly written statement of your intention.

Spread Some Magic

If you have like-minded friends, spread some magic and happiness by writing them a letter in the Witches' alphabet, which you can either mail to them or share with them in a photo. Choose your words carefully, because they're powerful. Try sticking to positive, inspiring messages and well wishes.

If you use snail mail, you can add corresponding herbs or objects to the envelope, making for a special magical treat. When your friend deciphers your note, they'll get multiple benefits: an unexpected witchy surprise, a meaningful gift, and the magic you've sent their way. They'll also probably have fun decoding your message. If you have an online group of magical friends, you can spread positivity around by writing a short personal message to each person in the Theban script. Photograph each note and send it directly to them to decipher.

Despite existing for centuries and being closely examined by many occultists and scholars, the Theban alphabet remains largely a mystery. While it's possible that we may never know the true reason it was invented, that shadowy obscurity surrounding it is perhaps its most powerful quality. The unknown gives us space to be freely creative with the ancient cipher, giving it new meanings and uses as we go, lending it more collective power and energy all the time. It's interesting to wonder if in two hundred years people will still be puzzling over this ancient alphabet, called to the symbols by the same whispers of the unknown, the esoteric and the mystical that have fascinated occultists, Witches, and magicians for centuries before them.

Resource

Jenkins, Greg. *The Theban Oracle: Discover the Magic of the Ancient Alphabet That Changes Lives.* San Francisco, CA: Weiser Books, 2014. See chapters 1 and 2.

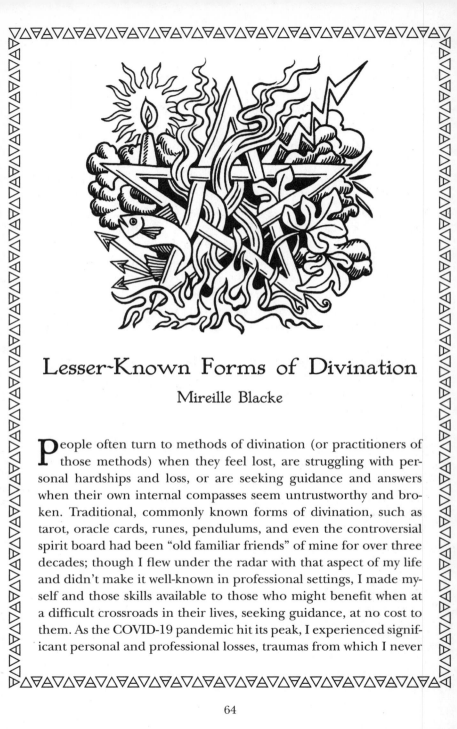

Lesser-Known Forms of Divination

Mireille Blacke

People often turn to methods of divination (or practitioners of those methods) when they feel lost, are struggling with personal hardships and loss, or are seeking guidance and answers when their own internal compasses seem untrustworthy and broken. Traditional, commonly known forms of divination, such as tarot, oracle cards, runes, pendulums, and even the controversial spirit board had been "old familiar friends" of mine for over three decades; though I flew under the radar with that aspect of my life and didn't make it well-known in professional settings, I made myself and those skills available to those who might benefit when at a difficult crossroads in their lives, seeking guidance, at no cost to them. As the COVID-19 pandemic hit its peak, I experienced significant personal and professional losses, traumas from which I never expected to recover. After the summer of 2020, I withdrew, turned my back on those "friends" and the world in general, because I was broken in many ways, felt physically and mentally exhausted, and needed to heal.

Luckily, true friends are there for you in challenging situations like the one I described, but we may not recognize this without the benefit of hindsight and the time that allows us to eventually gain this perspective. In the moment, we may be too overwhelmed to appreciate those around us.

A year later, in the early summer of 2021, as I began to regain confidence and apply for jobs, my older cousin Joe Lantiere died unexpectedly. He was the only family member of mine who shared certain traits with me. Joe was an openly practicing Witch in our family of Roman Catholics, a copious writer of offbeat topics, a Mensa member, and someone who followed his own eclectic path. He balanced science, logic, and skepticism with a penchant for artistic flair and wit. He non-judgmentally encouraged me to do the same, always. This one hurt. He'd influenced a great many creative minds in the Wiccan/Pagan community who took his loss to heart, and many of us are still processing that he's physically gone. It was Joe who introduced me to the dark night of the soul concept in my early twenties and helped shape my spiritual growth in Wicca and Paganism. This was more than a "family" thing; this was a soul connection, and I appreciated him greatly. But I wasn't sure if he knew that when he died; this greatly bothered me. It didn't take long before I was comforted in that regard.

In researching this topic, I rediscovered the tutorial Joe wrote on divination with paper clips (chromoclipmancy), which is now out of print. I do mean "rediscover" in the literal sense: when applying for one particular open position, I needed to reference an old job description, and being a packrat like Joe, I knew I had the information printed in some long-forgotten storage containers in the basement of my mother's house. "Some" is an understatement; it was more like fifty to sixty white, unlabeled banker's boxes—an overwhelming undertaking, especially considering my state of mind and the pressure I felt to find a job. Facing the wall of boxes I hadn't thought of in decades, I didn't know where to start or whether I should bother trying: I felt worthless after everything that had happened. I decided to leave it to the universe and selected one random box. I pulled the cover off that one box for guidance on where to go from there, fully expecting to give up after opening it and finding it full of nothing but meaningless and outdated papers. Instead, I removed the cover and found first an empty interoffice envelope addressed to "Joe Lantiere" with his old chromoclipmancy tutorial underneath it, where they had no business being, on top of a colorful, outdated stack of travel brochures for my favorite city in the world, New Orleans. I smiled through my tears and admitted that for an evidence-based individual, I viewed this "as a sign" that I was on the right track (an example of transataumancy, or things accidentally seen or heard). My reasoning? I was applying for an office job, but it was in radio, the industry I left decades earlier but adored as much as my beloved New Orleans. I took this as direction to move to the box directly behind this one and found the job description information I was actually seeking that day, in addition to many printed emails that Joe and I had sent back and forth to one another during the same time period (summer 2001, twenty years ago). They made me laugh and cry a bit as well. Take that as you will, but it was a comforting (and time-saving) experience.

Hollywood and media have popularized and misrepresented certain forms of divination, like tarot cards and fortune-telling with a crystal ball, to the point of ridicule and stereotype, while the Ouija board has become nefarious (but for the record, I don't advocate its use for divination purposes). Other common divination methods include palm reading (chiromancy), numerology, automatic writing, candle reading, coin divination (numismatomancy, such as the popular I Ching), flower reading (anthomancy/floromancy), tea leaf reading (tasseomancy), and dream interpretation (oneiromancy).

There are also dozens of lesser-known and uncommon forms of divination that may be just as useful as the more popular methods. In fact, these lesser divination methods were often more handy and or convenient (e.g., food sources) for common people who sought insight or guidance in making challenging decisions about their lives. Such typical household items used for divination purposes include cheese (tyromancy), eggs (oomancy), ink (encromancy), coffee grounds (tasseomancy), flour (aleuromancy), and salt (alomancy). It's just as important today that lesser-known forms of divination do not fade into obscurity, as they can be just as useful, convenient, and affordable. It's not always necessary to delve deeply into a multi-layered tarot card reading or probe past lives, and there are times when you want to cut to the chase for a quicker answer and don't need a deep dive. These simpler techniques will get the job done, save you time, effort, and usually money.

Scrying, or gazing at a reflective surface, is more about tapping into your unconscious mind than about divination, but Hollywood and various forms of media have not helped the global perception of this ancient art of revelation. I'm including scrying in this article to clear up the misperception about it and because developing this skill (which is not easy) can improve your divination techniques, should you decide to pursue those. Because scrying involves a reflective surface, it can be done with the more common crystal, fire, mirror, smoke, water, and wine, or even a polished fingernail or toenail (onychomancy). Though scrying can be done with a crystal ball, the Hollywood portrayal of using it for divination purposes is inaccurate and cost-ineffective, as crystal balls are not inexpensive or low maintenance. However, scrying and divination can be more easily, affordably, and conveniently accomplished using ink, in two steps.

Ink (Encromancy)

Because scrying involves the use of a reflective surface, the point of using black ink is to create the appearance of a black mirror. (An obsidian stone would also be an acceptable substitute for this purpose.) It's important to begin with a clear mind, in a calm setting of your choice. In a darkened room, with a single light source to provide a point of reflection, fill a shallow bowl slowly with drops of black ink. Images may appear to you, though they may be hazy, lacking clarity. As with any skill, scrying requires practice, patience, and commitment over time. A secondary option is to drop ink into the bowl of water and interpret patterns that may emerge.

Relaxation is also key for practicing encromancy, or divination with ink stains. (Those who recall the famous Rorschach inkblot tests should find this divination method familiar.) This technique requires a clean sheet of white paper, and most encromancers recommend using Indian ink for best results. Specific encromancy techniques vary. For some, you'll fold the white paper length-wise, writing the name of the person with the question on each side of the paper. Depending on the reader's preference, slowly and carefully spill three, seven, or thirteen inkblots onto the paper, allowing the ink to spread onto the unwrinkled paper and dry. Other readers might pour the ink, then fold the paper into four sections, press with the non-dominant hand, and unfold after several minutes. Either way, after the ink dries, the reader will proceed to interpret the shapes of the stains formed on the paper. As with many other divination methods, the shapes formed by the ink stains provide the reader with indications of the past or future. Though potentially messy, encromancy seems to be another useful, though less practiced, divination option.

Song Lyrics (Shufflemancy)

Divination using books is known as bibliomancy and is a common practice. It involves first selecting a book (the Bible, book of poetry, or one of your choice) to which you feel a connection. Pose the question for which you seek an answer, letting your chosen book open to a random page. You may choose to close your eyes when you do this, and use your finger to select a random sentence. The sentence you select is the answer to your posed question. Bibliomancy may be modernized as "shufflemancy" using an iPod, laptop, car radio (terrestrial or satellite), or mobile phone with a playlist, contingent upon access to a shuffle function, writes Icy Sedgwick. Once you ask your question, hit shuffle. Your answer will be the first verse of lyrics to the first song that follows your question.

Cheese (Tyromancy)

There are a number of ways to use cheese as a divination tool, depending on your available cheese selection and personal preferences. Cheese divination method details aren't historically well-documented, but deductive reasoning can be applied along with some common sense. After making your intentions clear, view the depth, size, and shapes of the holes in the cheese for meaning. For example, a large, deep heart shape could indicate a significant relationship or lasting love, or the opposite might indicate the lack thereof. Certain shapes and holes in the cheese may resemble initials, which could provide answers as well, writes Zach Seemayer. Divining with cheese was also accomplished by leaving answers to questions on different pieces and watching for mold to grow over time. The piece of cheese on which the mold grew first would eventually provide the answer. While I don't find this concept particularly appetizing, I can understand how it may have developed over time, especially during the Middle Ages, when form and function were as much about adaptability and survival as they were about dealing with day-to-day boredom and facing the realities of the human condition.

Eggs (Oomancy)

When I've mentioned egg divination to people, I've usually gotten double-takes as responses, and I suppose to some it may seem amusing. I appreciate the versatility of this category, though, as I found several subcategories with which I was unfamiliar. (Please see the further reading list at the end of this article.)

Historically, individuals who felt they'd been "hexed" sought relief from healers who confirmed their plight via egg divination. A number of egg-related techniques were used to understand the afflicted's circumstances, but today, oomancy generally involves interpreting shapes in the egg white as it floats in water, after focusing on the posed question or concern. Start the process by filling a clear bowl (or large glass) with warm water; be mindful to not overheat the fluid or "cook" the egg white. While you focus on your question, you'll also use a pin to open a tiny hole in the egg to allow the egg white only to slowly drip into the water in the bowl, explains the Association of Independent Readers and Rootworkers. Patterns will emerge in the bowl for you to interpret; be sure to gaze into the bowl or glass from all viewpoints (top, sides, underneath) to see if different angles offer you additional interpretations.

Salt (Alomancy)

One of the easiest and most accessible (but rarely used) divination methods involves salt (alomancy). For people looking for a yes/no answer to a question, the following technique is a quick option:

1. Place a small handful of loose, coarse salt in a pan of your choice on your stovetop, on a low heat. Cover the pan and keep heated for 15 minutes. (*Note: do not heat salt slabs or apply the salt directly to the stove or open flame. Protect your eyes and face.*)
2. Focus on your yes/no question.
3. According to alomancy lore, your answer is yes if the salt is slow to crackle or remains quiet on the stove. Your answer is no if the salt pops, snaps, or crackles loudly for a long time, shares *Psychic Sphere*.

Lesser-Known Forms of Divination

Method Using	Formal Name
Ants	Myrmomancy
Bamboo	Kau cim
Barley bread	Alphitomancy
Beans	Favomancy
Beetle tracks	Skatharomancy
Belly button/navel	Omphalomancy/omphilomancy
Archery/arrows	Belomancy
Blood	Hematomancy
Books of poetry	Rhapsodomancy
Burned incense/ash	Libanomancy
Burning straws with hot iron	Sideromancy
Sound of burning laurel leaves	Daphnomancy
Candle wax	Ceromancy
Chance animal encounters	Apantomancy
Cheese	Tyromancy
Clouds	Nephomancy
Coconut	Obi abata
Cowrie shells	Conchomancy
Dog(s) howling	Ololygmancy
Dust	Abacomancy
Eggs	Oomancy/ovamancy
Fallen wood	Xylomancy
Fashion/clothing	Stolisomancy
Fig leaves	Sycomancy
Fish behavior	Ichthyomancy
Flame shapes	Lampadomancy
Flour	Aleuromancy
Forehead lines	Metopomancy
Fossils, minerals	Oryctomancy
Frogs	Batraquomancy
Horse movements	Hippomancy

Method Using	Formal Name
Human urine	Urimancy
Ink	Encromancy
Japanese wooden sandals	Geta-uranai
Keys	Cleidomancy
Laughter	Geloscopy
Metal weights	Zygomancy
Nails (finger, toe)	Onychomancy/onixomancy
Needles/pins	Acutomancy
Oak or mistletoe	Dendromancy
Onion sprouts	Cromniomancy
Overheard words	Cledonomancy
Paperclips	Chromoclipmancy
Pearl casting	Margaritomancy
Pig bladders	Choriomancy
Rodents	Myomancy
Roosters	Alectryomancy
Rose petals, leaves	Phyllorhodomancy
Salt	Alomancy
Seeds in bird excrement	Stercomancy
Small objects	Micromancy
Smoke movement	Capnomancy
Smoke shapes	Turifumy
Snake movements	Ophiomancy
Song lyrics (random)	Shufflemancy
Stomach noises	Gastromancy
Swords/knives	Macharomancy
Tambourines	Tympana
Things accidentally seen or heard	Transataumancy
Thunder and lightning	Ceraunoscopy
Turtle shells, bones	Plastromancy/scapulimancy
Umbilical cord (knots)	Omphilomancy
Wheel tracks	Trochomancy

After I put this list together, it was empowering to review the amount of lesser-known divination options available, assuming a person is open to divination methods to begin with. I do emphasize choice here, for a reason. No matter which form of divination you might select, it's important to ask permission before implementing any divination techniques on anyone else's behalf. It may be tempting to pry into other people's business, but it's not ethical, and it's a slippery slope.

My cousin Joe's legacy will continue to positively impact people now just as he did over the course of his life, one by one, whether he knew it or not. In reading this article, you've now become one of the people he's indirectly influenced, and that connects us. He'd get a kick out of that but also tell me I was a dork for mentioning it.

For whatever reason, I was offered and accepted the job for which I applied when I "accidentally" found Joe's chromocliptomancy tutorial and empty interoffice mailer that day in early summer 2021. Joe would raise an eyebrow of concern if I assumed every random paper clip I found on the floor meant something significant or was a sign from Joe about something. There are people who can take methods of divination to the extreme (whether they know it's divination or not) and live their lives based on "signs" taken from songs played at random on the radio or strategic timing of a license plate, and I don't believe such complete abandonment of free will is psychologically healthy. But I also understand the appeal of letting the universe take the wheel and guide you when life has become too much, and every step we take feels like we're landing three steps back.

For me, using common or lesser forms of divination does not mean laying down my free will; we still have the ability to choose and make decisions about the paths we take in our lives. Divination, and particularly the lesser-known forms that involve

A LITTLE BIT OF MAGIC

In geta-uranai, a Japanese wooden sandal is kicked into the air to predict the weather; the sandal's landing facing up indicates clear skies ahead, on its side suggests clouds, and facing down predicts rain or poor weather.

more common, accessible techniques and items, is just available to help us gain insight into those pathways and shine a light when we're in the darker parts of the journey, or when the streetlamps temporarily dim. For those dark nights of the soul, divination may be one of those true friends you didn't realize you had that provides you with such a light when you can't provide it for yourself. Like my dear cousin, you may have the chance to provide that light for someone else to change or even save their lives.

You never know. It may not be a light; it may just be a paper clip. But that may be enough.

Thank you, Joe.

Resources

"Alomancy." *Psychic Sphere* (blog). Accessed August 21, 2021. https://www.psychic-sphere.com/divination/alomancy/.

Association of Independent Readers and Rootworkers. "Egg Divination." Accessed August 21, 2021. http://www.readersandrootworkers.org/wiki/Category:Egg_Divination.

"Divination by Ink Stains." Accessed August 24, 2021. https://tarotsi.net/oracle-encromancy.html.

Powers, Serena. "Unusual Methods of Divination and Fortune Telling. Serena's Guide to Divination." Accessed August 21, 2021. https://www.serenapowers.com/unusual.html.

Sedgwick, Icy. "Fortune-Telling Made Easy: 4 Strange Forms of Divination." March 21, 2020. https://www.icysedgwick.com/fortune-telling-2/.

Seemayer, Zach. "Strange Methods of Predicting the Future That Put Tarot Cards to Shame." Ranker. May 18, 2021. https://www.ranker.com/list/strangest-divination-methods/zach-seemayer.

Further Reading

Casas, Starr. *Divination Conjure Style*. Newburyport, MA: Weiser, 2019.

Dean, Liz. *Nature's Hidden Oracles*. London: Godsfield, 2021.

Verner-Bonds, Lillian. *Divination Dictionary*. New York: Sterling Ethos, 2020.

The Magic of Scent

Suzanne Ress

Have you ever caught a stray whiff of a stranger's perfume and were instantly reminded of someone else close to you, or even of yourself at an earlier time? A rush of memories may ensue. That scent I had loved and worn back in my teens but had forgotten about? Just a hint of it will send my mind back! I'll suddenly remember my favorite clothes, my friends, what I spent my time doing, and, especially, my emotional and psychic states.

Have you ever walked into the home of someone you love but haven't seen for a while and been shot back into your former emotional groove by that sudden but unmistakable scent? Although my grandmother Martha died many years ago, I can still conjure up vivid memories of her just by smelling freshly perked coffee and aniseed cookies, which was what I smelled every time I entered her kitchen.

My father used a particular and no longer available brand of tooth-cleaning powder, which I got a faint whiff of when he kissed us kids goodbye each morning. My olfactory memory still recalls that scent. I can "think" how orange peel smells, as well as bread baking, peppermint candy, gasoline, burning leaves, freshly mown lawn, fresh asphalt, cut cucumbers, and on and on.

Smells and scents are invisible and can be ephemeral, but they are real, volatile molecules that travel in the air. Whether you are conscious of them or not, they can have a marked effect on your state of mind.

It is well known that canines have an excellent sense of smell, but many, if not most, other animals do too. This includes humans. Although we have far fewer functional smell receptors than a dog does, typically a human only occasionally consciously uses their sense of smell, perhaps not noticing scents unless they are particularly strong or unexpected. Nevertheless, scent is always around us and always has at least a subtle influence on us. Our sense of smell and its connection with our emotions and memory can be put to use in spellcasting and in general atmospheric magic.

Improve Your Scent Awareness

The first step in successfully using scent for magic is to become hyper aware of the odors around you in all your waking moments. Wherever you are at any time, take a minute or two to consciously smell the air. Notice and name all the scents you pick up. Naming odors helps you distinguish them more clearly in your mind.

At this moment, I am sitting in my living room with all the windows open. It is around the middle of the day, and what I smell is this: the tropical pineapple scent of the infuser on the table, a light rose smell coming from my hands from the scented cream I applied earlier, the distinct old-fashioned scent of boxwood bush coming from outside the window, the dusty smell of the sofa, the almost tarry smell of my notebook, and a light petrichor after-rain smell on the breeze (it rained about an hour ago). I have smelled all this without moving or making any effort.

Practice doing this exercise as often as you can. It is especially interesting to do this when you take a walk outdoors, as you will discover there is a huge variety of smells that constantly changes according to place, time, weather, and activities going on or having gone on there.

Another way to improve your awareness of scent is to purposely smell something while verbally repeating aloud several times what it smells like. Go through your spice cupboard and smell cinnamon saying, "Cinnamon, cinnamon, cinnamon," and then smell tarragon, nutmeg, and so on. Or go through your herb garden or your refrigerator and do the same thing. This will help etch your memory with specific smells and make it easier to recognize them when you encounter a smell that is a blend of several or many different scents.

Almost all scents are made up of a variety of osmotic molecules, which can make it more difficult to put your finger, or nose, on them and to understand what you are smelling.

Whenever possible, practice with and make use of real odors. Smell a patch of damp moss in the forest rather than a "moss" scented candle. Grate and inhale the scent of lemon rind rather than a bottled lemon essential oil. Bury your nose in a sweet climbing rose in full bloom rather than lighting a stick of rose incense. Freshly ground cinnamon bark is preferable to cinnamon extract. When you inhale these natural scents, try to clear your mind of any preconceptions and really smell what is there. Of course, there are many perfumes we cannot smell first-hand because their source isn't readily available. Sandalwood, myrrh, frankincense, patchouli, and many other first-hand fragrances are too exotic or rare to come by easily. In these cases, a good-quality essential oil will be the best choice. Many scented candles, soaps, and incenses contain artificial laboratory-created scents, which can be slightly, or widely, off base.

Another excellent exercise to improve your "scentsibility" is to have someone else present you with an array of samples one at a time while you are blindfolded. In this exercise it is best to name whatever odors your nose picks out rather than try to figure out what the smelt object actually is. A cut string bean may smell green and leafy, sweetly floral, and slightly pungent like sauerkraut, for example. Be attentive not to have washed your hands with any kind of scented soap nor to have used scented hand cream.

The human brain's limbic system, where memories are stored, also processes smells. No other of our senses has this direct neurological connection. Odors can affect our moods and behaviors only if we have previously been in contact with that odor and can consciously or subconsciously associate it with an event, place, person, or other memory. Pleasant environmental odors are better than odorless environments in improving people's moods and performance, while unpleasant odors have a negative impact on mood and performance.

It is important to be aware of how particular odors affect you. Then it is hit or miss using these same odors to affect others, but you'll learn as you go. Associating a particular scent with peacefulness by meditating while smelling it can make it possible to elicit a feeling of peacefulness just by smelling that scent without meditating. Human emotions arise and develop in the part of the brain called the amygdala, which is the same area of the brain that processes and contains memories and our sense of smell. Olfactory sense, emotion, and memory are very much interwoven as a result. Just like associating a passer-by's perfume with someone you have known and loved and then experiencing a rush of feeling and memory, we can use scent in the opposite direction. That is, we

A Little Bit of Magic

IN ADDITION TO DOGS, FRUIT FLIES, WORMS, AND BEES HAVE BEEN USED FOR THEIR SENSE OF SMELL IN DETECTING VARIOUS CANCERS AND COVID-19.

can purposely create desirable associations with a particular scent, which we will be able to re-experience anytime afterward by merely smelling that scent. This can be extremely useful in magic spell-work, as it often relies on repeating an affirmation many times, over a period of time, in order to make one's desire manifest.

Trigeminal Stimulation

Different smells have different feels to them. Mint smells cool, but coolness is a feeling, not a smell. Ammonia has a burning feel, cinnamon feels warm, and onions feel sharp. These feelings associated with odors are produced by the trigeminal system, which is a system of temperature-sensitive feeling and pain fibers in our nose and face. This system is what makes you cry when you cut onions, what creates the burning sensation when you eat very spicy hot peppers, and why ground pepper can make you sneeze. As a result, for example, a scent like mint or menthol is usually subconsciously associated with freshness.

Scents have the power to relax, soothe, excite, or put us in a positive or negative mood, depending on our previous memory-related associations with them. Lavender scent in itself will not create a sensation of tranquility and relaxation unless you personally have had tranquil and relaxing memory associations with it. This is quite likely, though, as lavender is a common ingredient in calming teas and soothing bath products, which consciously you may not have fully been aware of.

After spending some days or weeks becoming ever more aware of odors and scents in the air and emanating from things, and from beings around you, you will be ready to try some scent magic.

Here are some scent associations of my own, but it is imperative that you be inventive and create your individual scent associations for whatever spell you wish to cast, or it will not work!

Riches: Ginger, basil, mint
Everlasting Love: Rose, vanilla, musk
Increased Energy: Orange, clove
Improved Health: Apple, fern, moss

The most important thing to remember when developing a scent for magic is that the scent must not carry any previous memory associations with it. If you want to cast a spell for increased riches, the scent you use can smell like money, as mine does, or it can have a different scent unrelated to money, something that smells rich to you. Perhaps a buttery chocolate-vanilla spice cake smell or a rich, fruity, mango-banana-melon scent will epitomize riches for you.

Scents for magic are best made up using essential oils. These can become rather expensive, so start off by acquiring and using just a few (one to three) essential oils, and increase your collection gradually as needed. The most important thing to remember when creating a magic scent is that it must not carry any previous conflicting associations for you!

The Scent of Richness Spell

Make sure you will not be disturbed. Go to your special sacred place with a plain white candle, a lighter, and your chosen scent oil blend, and spend some time sitting quietly and breathing deeply until you are completely relaxed. Massage a few drops of your scent oil into the candle using both of your hands. Set the candle in a secure holder, light it, and gently massage another drop of scent oil into your hands. Say aloud as the candle burns, "My wealth increases. My life is filled with riches. My hands are full of wealth. I am rich." Repeat these lines over and over many times while watching the candle burn and smelling the scent on your hands. At the same time, visualize yourself having all the riches you desire. Imagine yourself surrounded by piles of gold and coins, rolling in a mountain of paper money, inhabiting a palace, or whatever works for you. Do not go on with your repetition and your imagery so long that you no longer notice the scent of richness. When this begins to happen, extinguish the candle, for the spell is complete.

When you are sure the candle's wick is cool, carefully wrap the candle in a square of fabric. Bandanas are good for this. Tuck it away somewhere hidden. Wash your hands thoroughly several times over. Avoid smelling your richness essential oil for two days. On the third day, in a moment of complete relaxation, go to your sacred space and take several whiffs of your richness oil, affirming, "I am wealthy; my life is filled with riches."

Repeat this procedure three more times. After this, if it should occur to you to be feeling poor, take a whiff of your richness oil and see what happens.

Use this same technique—changing the scent oil, your verbal affirmations, and your visualization—to cast scent magic spells for everlasting love, increased energy, success at work or school, improved health, a more exciting sex life, safe travels, or whatever else you want. Any scent spell can be done in solitaire or with a partner or a group as long as all people participating agree on the scent.

A few drops of your magic scent oil can also be vaporized in a diffuser, for subtle environmental magic, at opportune moments.

Scent magic will open a part of your brain you may not have realized you had. Enjoy the wonders of the osmosphere! Blessed be!

Selected Resources

"Flies, Worms and Bees Could Help Detect Illness." *Economist*, July 28, 2021. https://www.economist.com/science-and-technology /2021/07/28/flies-worms-and-bees-could-help-detect-illness.

Herz, Rachel. *The Scent of Desire*. New York: Harper Perennial, 2007.

McGee, Harold. *Nose Dive*. New York: Penguin, 2020.

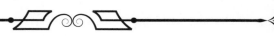

Nonverbal Quarter Calls

Elizabeth Barrette

Rituals customarily begin by defining and purifying the space. This includes calling the quarters or other anchor points, such as the Three Realms in a Celtic circle. Most of the time, people call the quarters with verbal invocations. These can be scripted or spontaneous. Many variations exist in print and online.

Challenges and Limits

Typical verbal invocations don't work as well in all situations. There are many reasons why this can happen. First, there are physical reasons, like people who have speech impairments, mouth injuries, or a sore throat that day. Another cluster of physical issues includes poor vision that makes it hard to read from a page and poor dexterity that prevents a person from handling script pages easily. Mental limitations include difficulty memorizing or ad libbing lines, low or no reading skill, difficulty reading aloud, and foreign language limitations. Social and emotional challenges range from shyness to anxiety, fear of public speaking, and so on. Some limitations, like stuttering and slurring, could be physical or mental and often get worse under stress. Sometimes people who can speak prefer not to, if they find their voice displeasing or unreliable, so they substitute another method.

There are other types of issue that can make a spoken invocation difficult or impossible. In most cases, the ritual designer doesn't need to know *why* the limitation exists, just a enough to compose a ritual that will work around it. Encourage people to mention if they need accommodations, but remember they're not obligated to share that. Conversely, if you have a limitation but choose not to disclose it, then you can't fairly complain should the ritual not suit your needs.

Another category of reasons to use nonverbal quarter calls is situational. Verbal invocations work best in reasonably quiet, close circles. If the environment is noisy—whether because of cars or cicadas or something else—then it can drown out key words and make the ritual hard to understand. It's actually possible to do an entire ritual without saying a word, and our coven has done it, but that does take more careful planning. Far more often, we've had to deal with wind strong enough to blow out candles and make pages impossible to read. On one particularly obnoxious occasion, we had a time-sensitive ritual that needed to be done at a specific time in a specific location, but the weather was blustery and spitting rain. We gave up on our flapping pages and just improvised.

A large circle poses different challenges. Once you get beyond about a dozen people, it becomes harder to hear clearly. Shouting risks losing your voice, and electronic amplifiers are iffy at best in magical contexts. So the more you can do that doesn't require people to parse words, the easier it will be for distant participants to follow the process. When a ritual gets really big—a hundred or more people—then you start running into issues where people can't even *see* clearly what's going on. With a large circle, or other situational issues, think about which nonverbal quarter calls will enable everyone to understand them easily.

Finally, there's one magical reason for using alternative calls, and that relates to the energy itself. Remember "to know, to will, to dare, and to keep silent." There is a lot of power in silence. If you're doing a ritual with primal energies or one about secrecy or some other congruent theme, then conducting a silent or at least wordless ritual can greatly enhance the effects. My coven has done this a few time for different purposes, and it is both magical and memorable.

Inclusivity and Accommodations

You can get around all sorts of personal limitations and bothersome conditions by using nonverbal quarter calls. Ideally, a coven

should collect a range of calls and other techniques. Then they always have something suitable and can improvise easily if situations change.

Inclusivity in ritual design allows all interested members to participate. However, it also offers other benefits. It assures members that they can keep participating if they later develop issues, like if an older Witch suffers a stroke and winds up with slurred speech. It challenges liturgists to compose new rituals to accommodate different needs and circumstances, rather than using the same scripts or techniques over and over.

Some of our most interesting rituals have grown out of inclusivity. We've held rituals with a blind person, a wheelchair user, someone who couldn't stand for a long time, people of a very wide range of ages, and so on. The idea of nonverbal quarter calls came when we acquired a new musical instrument that I really wanted to try out in ritual, and at the same time we had some coven members who could read aloud but weren't very confident with it. So I hit

on the idea of musical quarter calls instead, which turned out to be both fun and powerful.

You can use different patterns for adapting quarter calls. Usually, it is least obtrusive to use the same method to call all the quarters (e.g., all musical or all gestural) or to use a different method for each quarter (e.g., flute playing for east, candle lighting for south, water sprinkling for west, rock balancing for north) than to substitute just one quarter (e.g., flute for east but spoken verses for the other three). However, ask the people involved. Some folks may prefer a minimalist approach, changing only what absolutely needs to be changed, rather than changing the whole set.

Consider also whether the issues you face are temporary or permanent; progressive, static, or improving; and consistent or variable. This will influence which accommodations you choose and how long you need them. A split lip will heal in a few weeks, a speech impediment might improve slowly with therapy, but a vision impairment is typically permanent. For a temporary limitation, simple methods that require no special equipment will likely suffice. For a permanent limitation or one that affects multiple people, you might want to invest in something more substantial. If you're dealing with progressive or variable challenges, you'll need more flexibility, so try to include multiple options that you can deploy quickly at need. We have found it very useful to have modular or adaptable ritual scripts to account for things like unpredictable weather or variable health.

Nonverbal Quarter Calls

Nonverbal quarter calls come in a wide range of styles. This includes anything that is not made of actual words. Some of the techniques are silent, while others use sound. Only a few require people to produce the sound; most take a different approach altogether.

It's a good idea to collect tools or at least descriptions for nonverbal quarter calls. Items such as musical instruments or signs can be kept in a basket or a cabinet alongside other coven equipment.

Descriptions of nonverbal quarter calls and a collection of past rituals using them can go in a binder or be kept in computer files. Lots of people like to use both. We keep files of previous rituals, but we also have a big binder of stuff that we can flip through for inspiration while planning a ritual.

Let's take a look at some of the options people can use for non-verbal quarter calls.

Animal Sounds

These can be made in at least three different ways. People can mimic them vocally, which is the most personable. You can play recordings, which gives you the widest range of possibilities, as many animal sounds are available. You can use objects to create the sounds. In addition to actual animal calls for sale in wilderness stores, some musical instruments or other objects make animalistic sounds. A croaker is a wooden instrument often shaped like a frog with ridges on its back; when rubbed with a stick, it makes a sound like a frog or a cricket. If you have people who have some vocal ability, they can use the mimic option. If not, they'll need to choose one of the other methods instead.

Animals customarily relate to the elements and thence the quarters. Birds and other fliers correspond with air and east. Predators, spined or venomous creatures, and desert wildlife correspond with fire and south. Aquatic and amphibious animals correspond to water and west. Burrowing creatures as well as big heavy ones correspond to earth and north. If you are using a different system, like Asian or Native American ones, you will need to look up the elemental, directional, and animal correspondences within that system.

Augmentative and Alternative Communication

This spans a wide range of tools and techniques to assist with or substitute for verbal speech, ranging from simple signboards to complex computer programs. While these are most often used by

people with disabilities, they also work in many other situations where speech is unavailable or simply not the best approach.

Among the most helpful tools in this context is the use of signboards. You can quickly make paper signs for each of the quarters. If the limitation is long-term, a point card of multiple words or images relating to ritual actions may be worthwhile for discussing Pagan activities. A number of Pagan companies make batik, handpainted, or tie-dyed banners of the elements, quarters, deities, and other figures. If you have a big enough sign or banner for each quarter, this method can work well even over fairly large distances. Some crafters sell banner holders that stand on or stick into the ground, allowing the banner to serve as a marker for its quarter throughout the ritual. For a coven with permanent limitations, or for very large groups, these may be worthwhile investments, as they are much more durable and beautiful than a paper signboard.

Dance

Cultures from around the world have their own dance traditions. This has many applications in calling quarters. Dance requires no vocalizations or even music, although it often combines with music. Each caller may do a different dance, or they may use the same one. Particularly useful in large groups is to have every person in a quadrant of the circle perform the same dance, rather than just a single person calling each quarter. You can draw dances from cultures living in the east, south, west, and north. If you're standing on a hard, smooth surface and the callers wear hard-soled shoes, you can borrow some basic techniques from tap, clog, step, or other rhythmic dances to click out a pattern of sounds against the ground. Some cultures even have dances specially designed for spiritual use. For instance, in the African and diaspora traditions, each orisha has their own musical rhythms and dance steps. If you're dealing with limitations beyond verbal ones, then adaptive dance offers many options for dancing in a chair, with a wheelchair, on crutches, and so forth.

Gestures and Pantomime

These are meaningful motions that are not actually words. (See sign languages on page 90.) Some magical traditions already have specific gestures that are used in ritual. For example, there are invoking and banishing pentacles along with one for each of the four elements, and thus the directions based on correspondences. Some chants, like "Earth My Body," also have their own gestures relating to the four elements.

While a gesture can be static, pantomime is a motion that mimics doing something. Examples include blowing air, lighting a fire, dipping water, or digging a hole in the earth. Think about the game of charades and you can easily imagine many types of pantomime to enrich your rituals. Pantomime is especially valuable because it connects to the deep history of the Sacred Clown through the mime tradition, and the Jester/Juggler/Magician figure in magical and ordinary cards. If you want to give someone a whole, major role in a ritual that has no spoken lines, this is a great choice.

Incense

Incense comes in a variety of forms, including stick, cone, and loose. The first two work alone, whereas loose incense gets sprinkled over hot charcoal. Indoors, use a mild incense like the Japanese woodless sticks. Outdoors, consider stronger things like frankincense and myrrh resin on charcoal. Incense is another tool that works great in large rituals, because it's so affordable that you can give everyone their own stick if you want. You can also get giant incense sticks for outdoor use if you prefer one per quarter. There are hundreds of varieties, so it's easy to find some that match the elements, directions, or even deities if you like to invoke a different one in each quarter.

Mudras

Yoga for your hands! These are patterns you make with your fingers, hands, and arms to direct energy and symbolize concepts. They come from Hindu tradition, just like full-body yoga. Mudras

exist for the four classical elements plus akasha, or spirit, along with many deities and other themes. These work very well in small, quiet rituals and for people with disabilities that would make more vigorous methods a challenge.

Music

This can be used in two ways: live or recorded. Live gives you more energy; recorded gives you more options. Typically, woodwinds are for air and east, brass for fire and south, strings for water and west, and percussion for earth and north. However, some instruments are unusual and clearly cross these lines. Both a sea drum and a rainstick are technically percussion, but because they make water sounds, they belong in the west. It's good for a coven to collect

instruments that are easy to play, like a recorder for east or bongos for north. A cymbal, also technically percussion, has a brassy sound that works well for fire in the south.

Sacrificial Objects

Anything that is given to the elements will work. Powder or smoke can be scattered in the air. Flammable items can be tossed in a bonfire. Liquids can be poured on the ground. Many objects can be buried in or thumped on top of the earth. You can use a different method at each quarter or all the same but with the contents customized to different directions. This approach works best outdoors but can be done indoors if you have a fireplace or other suitable props.

Sign Languages

These are complete languages. Somatic languages tend to be more representational, while audio ones are more abstract. But it varies. American Sign Language is more concrete than English but less than Plains Indian Sign Language (a.k.a. Hand Talk). You can sign a whole invocation, or just one word, like *east* or *air*. Look at the signs and aim for ones that make sense to watchers who may not know the whole language.

Vocables and Other Vocalizations

Not all mouth sounds are words. Vocables and scat singing use nonsense syllables. Tonal chanting, like *OM*, is another option. These are good when people can make sounds but not words or when they have trouble with reading or memorization.

Conclusion

This should give you some inspiration on how to include nonverbal quarter calls in your rituals. You can use them to solve a variety of challenges. You can also use them just for fun, to add variety and energy to your work. Share the idea with your Pagan friends and see what else you can come up with!

The Magic Wand

Chic and S. Tabatha Cicero

In the entertainment sector today, it seems like you can't turn around without tripping over a magic wand somewhere. You see them in the movies, read about them in novels, or use them to save princesses and defeat villains in video games. You can purchase them at theme parks and Renaissance fairs for your whole family. Beautiful and sleek in their endless array of sizes and symbolism, magic wands are fascinating. But can you really just wave them around in the air, say a few enigmatic words, and expect the skies to open at your command?

What comes to mind when you hear the words *magic wand*? Do you think of a plain wooden stick imbued with natural power, or something more elaborate, like a baton covered in symbols and semi-precious gemstones? Do you picture a small handheld wand like the type wielded in the Harry Potter novels or a staff like Gandalf's? Why is the wand the universal implement in both magical tradition and modern practice? And is a wand really necessary for the performance of effective magic?

Sometimes referred to as rods, scepters, or staffs, magic wands have been used for millennia in spiritual practice. Magic staffs are generally longer like walking sticks, while wands or rods are shorter and often more tapered. Ornate scepters have long been used as symbols of authority or royalty, but they can also be charged with magical energy. Wands have been made from a variety of materials: bone, metal, stone, crystal, clay, and of course wood. Over 3,500 years ago, the Egyptians carved symbols into the tusks of the feared hippopotamus to create *apotropaic* (evil-averting) wands to protect their households from malevolent forces. Ancient Zoroastrian priests utilized a sacred bundle of tamarisk twigs called a *baresman* (or *barsom*) to create a link between the material and spiritual realms and to channel divine power. Ancient Roman *flamines* (fire

priests) carried them as well. Later Hellenistic texts such as the *Graeco-Egyptian Magical Paypri* contain several examples of the use of magical wands and staffs made of myrtle or other sacred woods to invoke deities. And some deities had their own magic wands: the goddess Circe with her "charming wand," the wine god Dionysus with his pine cone-topped *thyrsus*, and the messenger god Hermes with his serpent-entwined *caduceus*.

Wands were among several implements listed in medieval grimoires such as the *Key of Solomon* and were used by magicians and their assistants, but the primacy of the wand was emphasized by the fact that only the "master" (not his disciples) could carry it. The grimoires sometime refer to a separate staff which, like the shorter wand, was only to be used by the Master Magician.

The idea that the wand is an implement of the magician's will, as well as a symbol of the element of fire gained prominence during the Occult Revival of the nineteenth century, particularly through the writings of French occultist Éliphas Lévi. It was also during this time that the tarot suit of wands (*bastoni* in Italian and *batons* in French) became associated with the element of fire and *Atziluth*, the highest divine world of the Qabalists, as well as the fiery first letter *Yod* of the Tetragrammaton (YHVH, יהוה), the sacred name of God, whose true name is both unknown and unpronounceable.

The Hermetic Order of the Golden Dawn followed Lévi's lead in emphasizing the importance of the wand and its attribution to fire and will. The Order utilizes many different wands for various purposes, officers, and rituals, such as the Lotus Wand, the Phoenix Wand, and the Chief Adept's Winged Disk Wand, which are based on the Egyptian *Wadj,* the *Waas,* and the *Ur-uatchti* wands—scepters held by the gods as depicted in ancient papyrus scrolls. But the wand most often used by Golden Dawn magicians to invoke the powers of fire in their personal work is the Fire Wand, with a magnetized wire running through its core, painted in the colors of red and green and ornamented with various Hebrew names and sigils corresponding to the element of fire.

To answer a previous question: no, you can't just wave a wand, mutter an incantation, and expect the laws of physics to be suspended. Magic is a natural process, so it doesn't work against natural laws—it works with them. In magic a wand represents the magician's willpower or willed force. It denotes self-control and the disciplined ability to choose one's actions. Like a learned skill or a trained muscle, this willed force can be strengthened with practice. It must also have an intended goal, purpose, or point of focus that lies within the realm of possibility, because magic will always take the path of least resistance to achieve its stated goal in conformity with natural law.

A wand is used to extend the magician's will and add divine force to his or her natural magical strength. It can be employed whenever the magician wishes to focus and direct energy. Like any magical implement, the wand can be consecrated or charged with the symbolism and energy that it is designed to attract, giving it talismanic characteristics. And the possibilities for personalizing wands for specific purposes are endless.

Creating a Magic Wand

Once you've decide to craft a wand to aid you in your magical work, the next step is to determine what kind of wand would suit you best. Do you prefer something simple or ornate? Traditional or uniquely personal? What kind of symbolism do you want to add to it? What length would be best? Would you like to create a single, general purpose wand or a series of wands for specific energies?

If you have the time, energy, and inclination, you could make separate wands for individual planetary, zodiacal, or Qabalistic forces. There is no reason why you couldn't make a Jupiter Wand, a Solar Wand, a Capricorn Wand, or a Yesod Wand. You could even create wands for invoking specific angels or archangels: a Raphael Wand to invoke healing or a Gabriel Wand to invoke creativity, and so on.

Instructions for creating traditional wands from the medieval grimoires or standard Golden Dawn wands such as the Lotus Wand and the Fire Wand can be found in several books. Here we will describe how to make a simple, general purpose wand and a personalized Fire Wand.

A Simple Wooden Wand

Leonardo da Vinci is credited with saying, "Simplicity is the ultimate sophistication." Many magic workers would agree. To some, nothing can beat a simple wooden wand crafted from the branch of a tree. Although we personally have a wide assortment of elaborate Golden Dawn wands, some of our favorite wands include a plain almond wand given to us by a beloved teacher and a symbol-inscribed locust branch from a favorite childhood tree.

Consult the ever-useful *Cunningham's Encyclopedia of Magical Herbs* for the magical properties of different trees and chose the type of wood that best suits your needs. You may have trees near where you live that will cast off branches that you can use: aged branches will already have the bark off. For a fresh or cut branch you will need to peel off the bark before setting it aside on a flat surface to dry for at least three months.

It's always best to start work on any magical implement on the day and hour of the magical force that the implement is meant to represent. For the days, Sunday is associated with Sol, Monday with Luna, Tuesday with Mars, Wednesday with Mercury, Thursday with Jupiter, Friday with Venus, and Saturday with Saturn. (Energies of the zodiacal signs and the Qabalistic Sephiroth will be aligned with their planetary correspondences.) Planetary tables of the magical hours of the day and night are found in several books, including our own *Golden Dawn Magic*. If possible, work during the waxing Moon, avoid the waning Moon, and take a break from wand creation during Mercury retrograde. Never work on any implement when you are angry or upset—clear your mind with a meditation beforehand.

Sand the wood beginning with a coarse grade of sandpaper and finishing with a fine grade of sandpaper until the wand is smooth. You can forgo applying any symbolism if you are happy with the simple elegance of the natural wood. Or you can carve or etch whatever symbols you wish into the wand with a pocket knife or wood-burning tool. Carve or drill small holes into the wand where you can glue gemstones if desired. Apply a couple of coats of beeswax or teak oil to protect it and bring out the wood grain, sanding between coats. And voilà! Your wand is ready to be consecrated.

A Personalized Fire Wand

Since wands in general are attributed to the element of fire, it would be completely appropriate to craft a unique Hermetic-style Fire Wand according to your own preferences, symbolism, and ingenuity. It does not need to have a magnetized wire at its center, but it does need to speak to your personal conception of fiery energy.

You can start by acquiring a ¾-inch diameter dowel, cut to a length somewhere between 12 to 20 inches. Lumber yards usually offer these in pine, oak, and poplar. Sand and apply two or three coats of primer white paint to the dowel, sanding between each coat. Next, determine what symbolism you would like to add to it. The following table provides a list of names, symbols, and materials that you can draw upon for this purpose.

Correspondences of Fire

Godname of Fire: Elohim (Hebrew, meaning "the Gods")

Archangel of Fire: Michael (Hebrew, meaning "He who is like God")

Angel of Fire: Ariel (Hebrew, meaning "Lion of God")

Ruler of Fire: Seraph (Hebrew, meaning "Flaming One")

Zodiacal Signs: Aries, Leo, Sagittarius

Tarot Cards: Judgement (with Emperor, Strength, and Temperance for the signs)

Hebrew Letters: Yod (for fire in general) with *Heh, Teth,* and *Samekh* for the signs

Planets: Mars, Sol

Colors of the Fire Signs: Aries = Red, Leo = Yellow, Sagittarius = Blue

Angel of the Fire Signs: Hitsael

Sephiroth: Chokmah, Geburah, Netzach

Deities of Fire: Nusku, Gerra, Gibil, Ishum, Sekmet, Bast, Horus, Mont, Re, Prometheus, Hephaestus, Vulcan, Ares, Mars, Hestia, Vesta, Agni, Pele, Ogun, Brigit, Aed

Animals: Ram, lion, cat, centaur, dragon, snake

Symbols: Upright triangle, pyramid, wand, torch, candle flame, arrow, lightning bolt, forge, flame with kindling

Metals: Iron, steel, gold, brass

Woods: Hazel, oak, almond, ash, cedar, ebony, poplar

Gemstones: Fire opal, ruby, garnet, bloodstone, pyrite, lodestone, meteorite

Fabrics: Leather, satin, lace, velvet

Choose whatever symbols and Names of Power you want to adorn your Fire Wand. Water-based acrylic paint works best for magical implements. You may paint the bulk of the wand red, since that is the primary color associated with fire. You can also paint some of the added symbolism in green, since green is the "flashing" or complementary color to red. (Be sure to paint the symbol in white first, then in green, or else the green will be absorbed by the red and turn muddy.)

For a wand that includes the astrological fire triplicity, divide the shaft of the wand into three equal parts and paint them in the colors of Aries (red with the symbol of the sign ♈ in flashing green), Leo (yellow with the symbol ♌ in flashing violet), and Sagittarius (blue ornamented with a flashing orange symbol ♐).

But if you want to add more complex symbolism to the wand, feel free to add whatever colors your creativity dictates. (You may wish to add the name of the angel Hitsael, which comes from the Hebrew letters associated with the three fire signs, *Heh, Teth,* and *Samekh,* combined with the divine suffix -*al,* indicating the angel is "of God"). Add your magical name to confirm the link between you and your wand.

There are several ways you can address the head of the wand. You can attach a separate piece of wood carved to represent a cone, a triangle, a pyramid, the head of a lion, dragon, or ram, and so on. A forged piece of metal or a gemstone attributed to fire could also make an impressive wand-head. Leather can be glued on for a comfortable handgrip.

Finish the painted portions of the wand by spraying on a couple coats of non-yellowing acrylic lacquer, taking care to cover any leather or gemstones with masking tape or painter's tape until the finish coat is completely dry. (Don't leave the masking tape on for more than twelve hours or the lacquer will make it sticky.) If you don't want lacquer, you can brush on a couple coats of clear-drying acrylic gloss gel medium.

Once your wand is finished, the next step is to consecrate it, charging it with fire energy and sacred purpose.

A Simple Consecration Ritual for Your Wand

If you have a personal temple or dedicated sacred space in your home, that's great. If not, don't sweat it! Any uncluttered tabletop, desktop, or dresser-top will do as a makeshift altar. Cover it with a cloth colored in a hue appropriate to the energy represented by the wand. For a Fire Wand, a red cloth is the natural choice. Green is the flashing color of red, so placing a circle of green cord, twine, or ribbon at the center of the red cloth will lend a visual and psychic vibration to your working. Have a stick of frankincense and a lighter ready to use. Place a red candle outside of circle, on the side farthest away from you. (If you can't use a real candle for safety reasons, due to rambunctious pets, etc., then use an LED candle: the electrical energy it uses to create light will still represent the force of fire.) Have a red linen or silk bag nearby for wrapping your wand. Place your wand in the center of the green circle.

To begin, sit or stand as appropriate for you. Start with slow rhythmic breathing to relax the mind and body. Inhale slowly to the count of one, then exhale slowly to the count of two. Focusing on a deep rhythmic breath is an effective way to shift the mind's awareness inward and tap into the inherent power of the Divine.

Next begin a course of breathing known in yoga as the Breath of Fire. This is a form of *pranayama*, or breath control, involving slow passive inhales and active exhales that are rapid and loud. Do this for at least thirty seconds before continuing. (Don't do the Breath of Fire if you have any heart, respiratory, or spinal issues.) Then relax and let your breathing return to normal.

If you were sitting, stand before the altar if able. Light the stick of incense. Begin to vibrate or intone the Name of Power *IAO* (pronounced EE-AH-OH in slow, long syllables). This trigram is the Western equivalent to the Eastern mantra *OM*, and the three letters refer to a triad of Egyptian deities Isis, Apophis, and Osiris—or the cycle of life, death, and rebirth. As you vibrate the name, visualize the figure of a triangle with its apex pointed toward the red candle. Trace the lines of this triangle clockwise directly over your wand with the stick of incense, starting from the top point. While tracing the first line, inhale deeply then slowly vibrate "*eee*." When tracing the second line intone "*aahh*." Trace the third line and vibrate "*oohh*." Trace the triangle and intone the name five times (as five is the number of Spirit). The figure of the upright triangle is the traditional Western symbol of fire, and tracing it in conjunction with the triad name will strengthen the connection between your wand and the divine energies that govern the manifest universe.

Hold the incense stick above the wand and say,

The heaven is above and the earth is beneath. And between the Light and the Darkness, the energies vibrate. I call upon the Divine Source of All, by the Majesty of the Divine and fiery Name of Power ELO-HIM, the Archangel of Fire MICHAEL, the Angel ARIEL, the Triad Angel HITSAEL, and the ruler SERAPH to bestow this present day and hour, and confirm their mystic and potent influence upon this Fire Wand, which I hereby dedicate to purity and Occult Work, and may its grasp strengthen me in the work of the Magic of Light! May it aid me in all things that require action, energy, stimulation, movement, vitality, transformation, and initializing force!

At this time, you may dedicate your wand to any personal deity you deem appropriate. Picture a glory of light encompassing your wand, charging it with divine light and the enlivening powers of fire. Allow as much time as you need before thanking any personal deities or angels invoked.

Finally, wrap your consecrated wand in the red cloth. When you feel that your ritual is completed, extinguish the candle and end the rite.

• • • ☽ • • •

Now what? Your wand is now ready for use in invoking (or banishing) any energies that have gone into its symbolism and consecration. Skill in ritual magic is gained through practice and diligence. The methods involved include clearing the mind of internal chatter, creating a positive alignment with deity, focused visualization, vibration of holy names, projection of willed force, and directed intension. Equipped with these powerful tools and techniques, your magical work will be kindled by your own creativity and inspiration.

Resources

Agrippa, Cornelius. *Three Books of Occult Philosophy*. Edited and annotated by Donald Tyson. St. Paul, MN: Llewellyn Publications, 1993.

Greer, John Michael. *The New Encyclopedia of the Occult*. Woodbury MN: Llewellyn Publications, 2003.

Hortwort, JD. "Making a Magickal Staff." In *Llewellyn's 2022 Magical Almanac*, 195–201. Woodbury MN: Llewellyn Publications, 2021.

MacLir, Alferian Gwydion. *Wandlore: The Art of Crafting the Ultimate Magical Tool*. Woodbury MN: Llewellyn Publications, 2012.

Mathers, S. L. MacGregor, ed. and trans. *The Key of Solomon the King*. York Beach, ME: Samuel Weiser, 1974.

Peterson, Joseph H. "The Magic Wand." Twilit Grotto: Archives of Western Esoterica. Last modified June 16, 2020. http://www.esoteric archives.com/wands/index.html.

Regardie, Israel. *How to Make and Use Talismans*. London: The Aquarian Press, 1972.

2023 Almanac

The Date

The date is used in numerological calculations that govern magical rites. Below is a calendar for 2023.

JANUARY						
1	2	3	4	5	6	7
8	9	10	11	12	13	14
15	16	17	18	19	20	21
22	23	24	25	26	27	28
29	30	31				

FEBRUARY						
			1	2	3	4
5	6	7	8	9	10	11
12	13	14	15	16	17	18
19	20	21	22	23	24	25
26	27	28				

MARCH						
		1	2	3	4	
5	6	7	8	9	10	11
12	13	14	15	16	17	18
19	20	21	22	23	24	25
26	27	28	29	30	31	

APRIL						
						1
2	3	4	5	6	7	8
9	10	11	12	13	14	15
16	17	18	19	20	21	22
23	24	25	26	27	28	29
30						

MAY						
	1	2	3	4	5	6
7	8	9	10	11	12	13
14	15	16	17	18	19	20
21	22	23	24	25	26	27
28	29	30	31			

JUNE						
				1	2	3
4	5	6	7	8	9	10
11	12	13	14	15	16	17
18	19	20	21	22	23	24
25	26	27	28	29	30	

JULY						
						1
2	3	4	5	6	7	8
9	10	11	12	13	14	15
16	17	18	19	20	21	22
23	24	25	26	27	28	29
30	31					

AUGUST						
		1	2	3	4	5
6	7	8	9	10	11	12
13	14	15	16	17	18	19
20	21	22	23	24	25	26
27	28	29	30	31		

SEPTEMBER						
					1	2
3	4	5	6	7	8	9
10	11	12	13	14	15	16
17	18	19	20	21	22	23
24	25	26	27	28	29	30

OCTOBER						
1	2	3	4	5	6	7
8	9	10	11	12	13	14
15	16	17	18	19	20	21
22	23	24	25	26	27	28
29	30	31				

NOVEMBER						
		1	2	3	4	
5	6	7	8	9	10	11
12	13	14	15	16	17	18
19	20	21	22	23	24	25
26	27	28	29	30		

DECEMBER						
					1	2
3	4	5	6	7	8	9
10	11	12	13	14	15	16
17	18	19	20	21	22	23
24	25	26	27	28	29	30
31						

The Day

Each day is ruled by a planet that possesses specific magical influences:

MONDAY (MOON): Peace, sleep, healing, compassion, friends, psychic awareness, purification, and fertility.

TUESDAY (MARS): Passion, sex, courage, aggression, and protection.

WEDNESDAY (MERCURY): The conscious mind, study, travel, divination, and wisdom.

THURSDAY (JUPITER): Expansion, money, prosperity, and generosity.

FRIDAY (VENUS): Love, friendship, reconciliation, and beauty.

SATURDAY (SATURN): Longevity, exorcism, endings, homes, and houses.

SUNDAY (SUN): Healing, spirituality, success, strength, and protection.

The Lunar Phase

The lunar phase is important in determining the best times for magic.

THE WAXING MOON (from the New Moon to the Full) is the ideal time for magic to draw things toward you.

THE FULL MOON is the time of greatest power.

THE WANING MOON (from the Full Moon to the New) is a time for study, meditation, and little magical work (except magic designed to banish harmful energies).

The Moon's Sign

The Moon continuously "moves" through the zodiac, from Aries to Pisces. Each sign possesses its own significance.

ARIES: Good for starting things, but lacks staying power. Things occur rapidly, but quickly pass. People tend to be argumentative and assertive.

TAURUS: Things begun now last the longest, tend to increase in value, and become hard to alter. Brings out appreciation for beauty and sensory experience.

GEMINI: Things begun now are easily changed by outside influence. Time for shortcuts, communication, games, and fun.

CANCER: Stimulates emotional rapport between people. Pinpoints need, supports growth and nurturance. Tends to domestic concerns.

LEO: Draws emphasis to the self, central ideas, or institutions, away from connections with others and other emotional needs. People tend to be melodramatic.

VIRGO: Favors accomplishment of details and commands from higher up. Focuses on health, hygiene, and daily schedules.

LIBRA: Favors cooperation, social activities, beautification of surroundings, balance, and partnership.

SCORPIO: Increases awareness of psychic power. Precipitates psychic crises and ends connections thoroughly. People tend to brood and become secretive.

SAGITTARIUS: Encourages flights of imagination and confidence. This is an adventurous, philosophical, and athletic Moon sign. Favors expansion and growth.

CAPRICORN: Develops strong structure. Focus on traditions, responsibilities, and obligations. A good time to set boundaries and rules.

AQUARIUS: Rebellious energy. Time to break habits and make abrupt changes. Personal freedom and individuality is the focus.

PISCES: The focus is on dreaming, nostalgia, intuition, and psychic impressions. A good time for spiritual or philanthropic activities.

Color and Incense of the Day

The color and incense for the day are based on information from *Personal Alchemy* by Amber Wolfe, and relate to the planet that rules each day. This information can be taken into consideration along with other factors when planning works of magic or when blending magic into mundane life. Please note that the incense selections listed are not hard and fast. See page 264 for a list of color correspondences. If you cannot find or do not like the incense listed for the day, choose a similar scent that appeals to you.

Holidays and Festivals

Holidays and festivals of many cultures, nations, and spiritual practices are listed throughout the year. The exact dates of many ancient festivals are difficult to determine; prevailing data has been used.

Time Zones

The times and dates of all astrological phenomena in this almanac are based on **Eastern Standard Time (EST)**. If you live outside of the Eastern time zone, you will need to make the following adjustments:

PACIFIC STANDARD TIME: Subtract three hours.

MOUNTAIN STANDARD TIME: Subtract two hours.

CENTRAL STANDARD TIME: Subtract one hour.

ALASKA: Subtract four hours.

HAWAII: Subtract five hours.

DAYLIGHT SAVING TIME (ALL ZONES): Add one hour.

Daylight Saving Time begins at 2 am on March 12, 2023, and ends at 2 am on November 5, 2023.

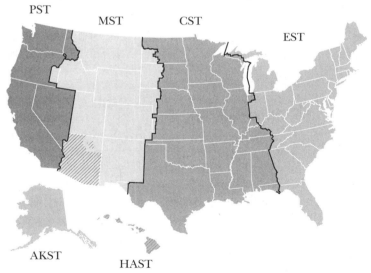

Please refer to a world time zone resource for time adjustments for locations outside the United States.

2023 Sabbats
and Full Moons

January 6	Cancer Full Moon 6:08 pm
February 2	Imbolc
February 5	Leo Full Moon 1:29 pm
March 7	Virgo Full Moon 7:40 am
March 20	Ostara (Spring Equinox)
April 6	Libra Full Moon 12:34 am
May 1	Beltane
May 5	Scorpio Full Moon 1:34 am
June 3	Sagittarius Full Moon 11:42 pm
June 21	Midsummer (Summer Solstice)
July 3	Capricorn Full Moon 7:39 am
August 1	Lammas
August 1	Aquarius Full Moon 2:32 pm
August 30	Pisces Blue Moon 9:36 pm
September 23	Mabon (Fall Equinox)
September 29	Aries Full Moon 5:58 pm
October 28	Taurus Full Moon 4:24 pm
October 31	Samhain
November 27	Gemini Full Moon 4:16 am
December 21	Yule (Winter Solstice)
December 26	Cancer Full Moon 7:33 pm

All times are Eastern Standard Time (EST)
or Eastern Daylight Time (EDT)

2023 Sabbats in the Southern Hemisphere

Because Earth's Northern and Southern Hemispheres experience opposite seasons at any given time, the season-based sabbats listed on the previous page and in this almanac section are not correct for those residing south of the equator. Listed here are the Southern Hemisphere sabbat dates for 2023:

February 2	Lammas
March 20	Mabon (Fall Equinox)
May 1	Samhain
June 21	Yule (Winter Solstice)
August 1	Imbolc
September 23	Ostara (Spring Equinox)
November 1	Beltane
December 21	Midsummer (Summer Solstice)

2023 Solar and Lunar Eclipses

Solar eclipse	April 20, 12:13 am	29° ♈ 50'
Lunar eclipse	May 5, 1:34 pm	14° ♏ 58'
Solar eclipse	October 14, 1:55 pm	21° ♎ 08'
Lunar eclipse	October 28, 4:24 pm	5° ♉ 09'

Two- and three-dimentional maps of the visibility range of an eclipse can often be found online leading up to the event. Even if it's not visible in your area, you can still draw on the energy of this astrological phenomenon.

2023 Energetic Forecast
by Charlie Rainbow Wolf

There's a lot going on this year! The overall vibe is one of hope, of finding a new path, of looking for meaning and direction. Magically, this is a good year for slowing down and going within. Spiritual practice is very important, so reestablish rituals and reconnect with those who are on the same wavelength. Spells associated with shamanic journeying could be particularly insightful. It's a time to explore the inner landscapes and to go deeper into your own psyche, but don't let that isolate you from others. What starts as contemplation could easily become preoccupation. Stay alone if you must, but at least stay connected with others in some way.

The tarot card for the year is the Chariot. This is a card of movement, of taking control, of seeing what's out there. This year has the potential to be very successful, but it's imperative that focus and tenacity are maintained. Supporting cards for the year are the sevens in the Minor Arcana. The Seven of Cups cautions against being indecisive or overindulgent, while the Seven of Pentacles encourages reflection and contemplation of goals being pursued. The Seven of Wands brings a fiery and passionate energy to challenges as they arise, and the Seven of Swords does caution that those challenges may come through deception or trickery—either from others or perhaps of your own making.

The numerology universal year number is a 7, supposedly quite a mystical number. There are fables about the seventh child of the seventh child, the seven wonders of the world, and seventh heaven. It's creative and philosophical and individualistic. It resonates with abstracts and philosophy and even mysticism. It questions the norm and often challenges it. One thing for sure, the number 7 is very enigmatic!

In the skies this year we've got quite the changes going on too. Pluto (a very slow-moving planet) will dip into Aquarius in March,

bringing a taste of what is to come for the next twenty years. Also in March, Saturn enters Pisces, staying there for until 2025. Both of these events bring slow but potentially profound changes. There's a unique eclipse over the equinox in April, which (according to NASA) starts out as an annular eclipse and then becomes total. Pay attention to where your focus lies at this time, for eclipses will always energize what is going on. This isn't the only eclipse, though; there are two solar and two lunar eclipses this year, as well as a Blue Moon. Let's take a closer look.

January

The year opens with a new calendar, a new numerology cycle, and a new vibe. January 1 has always been a good day for making those resolutions because it's the beginning of a new month, a new year, and a new numerological cycle. The universal month is number 8, a month for finding determination and purpose. The tarot card for this month is Strength, which goes hand in hand with staying focused and tenacious.

The Sun is in Capricorn for the first three weeks of this month, an earth sign. Earth signs are often represented by the turtle, who, according to some traditions, holds Earth on its back. The turtle's shell has thirteen segments; one for each Full Moon of the year. It's a very grounded and practical energy.

The Moon is waxing at the start of the new year, making it easier to stick to resolutions. The Full Moon in Cancer on the 6th could see emotions rising. The fourth quarter Moon in Libra on the 14th is a good time for seeking inner balance. A New Moon in Capricorn on the 21st brings a second chance to find determination for those resolutions. The second quarter Moon in Taurus on the 28th brings stability.

On the 12th, Mars stations direct in Gemini, followed by the end of Mercury retrograde in Capricorn on the 18th. Moving forward with plans should start to become easier, but patience is still

advised. Communication is less strained, particularly after the 21st. January 20th sees the Sun enter Aquarius, emphasizing individuality. Aquarius is an air sign, often represented by the butterfly, reflecting opportunities for transformation.

February

Things are fairly quiet in February. The Full Moon in Leo on the 5th brings heightened emotions that could give way to temper, so stay diligent. The fourth quarter Moon in Scorpio on the 13th is a good time for introspection. The New Moon on the 20th falls in Pisces, emphasizing a time for soul-searching. The Gemini second quarter Moon on the 27th emphasizes social connections.

The ruling tarot card for this month is the Hermit, bringing a time for reflection and contemplation. Numerologically, the month is a 9, a time for wrapping things up and preparing for what is yet to come. This is a good time for introspection and making plans to act on in the future.

On February 18th the Sun enters Pisces, heralding a creative time, but one when reality must be kept in check. Pisces is a water element, frequently associated with the frog. It's a good time for creativity and reflection. Mercury enters Aquarius on the 11th, which brings a social vibe but perhaps a bit of stubbornness to plans and interactions. On the 20th Venus enters Aries, adding passion and energy to activities and relationships. On the whole it's a fairly progressive month.

March

The first week of March ends with the Full Moon in Virgo; take care not to be too critical. The fourth quarter Moon in Sagittarius on the 14th is a good time for a heart-to-heart chat. The Aries New Moon on the 21st should see energy rising—well, it is the spring equinox, after all! The second quarter Moon in Cancer on the 28th draws attention to feelings and family matters.

The tarot card for the month of March is the Wheel of Fortune, which is associated with changeable energy. This is backed up by numerology, for the number for March is 1, the number of starting afresh. It's quite a Piscean month, with the Sun and Mercury being in Pisces at the start of the month, and Saturn entering Pisces on the 7th. It's a good time for spiritual pursuits, but don't get deluded.

Other planetary movement sees Venus entering Taurus on the 16th, where it is very comfortable and where relationships and careers could start to improve. Mercury enters Aries on the 19th, which is good for thinking out loud. The Sun moves into Aries on the 20th, a fire sign, sometimes associated with the passionate energy of the mythological thunderbird.

Pluto enters Aquarius for the first time on the 23rd, bringing a glimpse of the transformative energy that will eventually settle once he's finished bouncing back into Capricorn. This is a time for breaking down what has been established and finding solutions to old problems. On the 25th Mars enters into Cancer, infusing home life and traditions with fiery energy.

April

The Full Moon enters Libra on the 6th, bringing with it a sociable energy. This starts to mellow toward the last quarter Moon in Capricorn on the 13th. The big news this month is the New Moon eclipsing the Sun in Aries on the 20th. Solar eclipses expose things that have been hidden, and with this happening in Aries, the energy may lean toward the abrasive. Tenacity could lead to temper tantrums when things don't go according to plan. Patience is elusive, but it is also extra necessary at this time. Use this energy to close the door on what is no longer working and to seek out new beginnings. The 27th sees the second quarter Moon in Leo, another fire sign, and a time when energy is on the increase.

The tarot card for this month is Justice with a hint of the High Priestess's influence, bringing a wise reminder to keep all these energies in balance. The numerology is a master number 11, which embraces the newness of 1 with the duplicity of 2. Some real epiphanies may be experienced during this time.

The Sun enters Taurus on the 20th, bringing a more earthy and stable vibe to things. Taurus is an Earth (turtle) sign, and brings the power of both Theseus and the Minotaur. Also in April—on the 21st—Mercury stations retrograde in Taurus; this is not a time for making commitments, for things could become unnecessarily complicated.

May

The waxing Moon over Beltane brings heightened vitality that comes to a head on the 5th with the Full Moon in Scorpio, a wa-

ter sign that runs deep and full of passion. This is accentuated by the lunar eclipse. The fourth quarter Moon in Aquarius may bring solitude and a time for reflection. On the 19th the New Moon is in Taurus, and is a good time to initiate plans and projects. The second quarter in Virgo on the 27th should see cooperation, provided egos are held in check.

The tarot card for this month is the Hanged Man, with undertones from the Empress. This is a good month to choose what needs to be nurtured and what needs to be sacrificed in order to make things more fertile. Numerologically, May is a universal number 3, social and friendly but perhaps a bit superficial; avoid being taken in by pretty words.

The Sun enters Gemini on the 20th. This is an air sign, very mercurial, but there's a restless and changeable energy here. May sees Mercury station direct in Taurus on the 13th, and this is going to make it much easier to ground ideas and make them a reality. Jupiter enters Taurus on the 16th, adding to that positive but determined vibe. Mars enters Leo on the 20th, bringing all kinds of positive energy to social situations.

June

The Full Moon in Sagittarius on the 3rd brings an optimistic and philosophical energy, particularly when it comes to social interactions. The fourth quarter Moon on the 10th falls in Pisces, and is a time for walking the inner pathways rather than doing too much entertaining. The New Moon in Gemini on the 18th could well spark new plans or new connections with others, emphasized by the second quarter Moon in Libra on the 26th.

The tarot card for June is a card of transformation, the Death card. This is not anything to do with doom and gloom, though, and it is heavily influenced by the Emperor's wisdom; this is a chance for real growth. Numerology-wise, the month is quite karmic, ruled

by both 13 and 4. This brings a chance to stabilize your destiny, to go back to what is unfinished or what needs changing, and steer a new course.

The Sun enters Cancer on the 21st, the Summer Solstice. This is a time for gently connecting with others to observe the traditions and festivals of this period. Home and family may become important. On June 5th Venus enters into Leo, a grandiose placement for the planet of love and money. The last days of the month see Mercury—which has been in Gemini since the 11th—also enter Cancer, causing potential challenges between feeling and reason. Saturn turns retrograde on June 17th, and while this might impede things, it also brings a chance to create some stability around them. Saturn is slow moving and goes retrograde for about twenty weeks every year; it's something that is not particularly unusual, just a factor to consider when making any important life changes.

July

The Full Moon in Capricorn on the 3rd starts the month off on an industrious note. The Aries fourth quarter Moon on the 9th might bring some tensions as well as some challenges between wanting to be reserved and wanting to charge ahead. A New Moon in Cancer on the 17th could highlight that feeling of reserve, but by the time the second quarter Moon enters Scorpio on the 25th, emotions will seem stronger, even if not yet completely out in the open.

Temperance is the tarot card for July, and it brings a request for balance. Weigh all options before making any decisions. Choose goals carefully and find the reason and the motivation for attaining them. The universal month numerology is 5; if you believe in luck, this could prove to be quite a fortuitous month! There's also a bit of karmic debt around this month, so make sure to back up words with actions, acting with integrity at all times.

Astrologically, Mars enters Virgo on the 10th, bringing a sense of urgency to activities and plans. Mercury trades Cancer for Leo

on the 11th, and as the planet is moving direct, this bodes well for social activities, particularly the last week of the month. The Sun enters fiery Leo on the 22nd—the sign it rules—and it's very much at home here. Venus turns retrograde on the 22nd, so the next few weeks are not going to be the best times for romance or finances. Finally, Mercury jumps ahead of the Sun and enters into Virgo on the 28th, which should be good for seeing some substantial progress toward long-term goals.

August

August opens with the first Full Moon of the month, in the enigmatic Aquarius. The fourth quarter Moon in Taurus on the 8th brings a practical—although somewhat reserved—approach to things. A New Moon in Leo on the 17th might ask for extra patience, while the second quarter Moon in Sagittarius on the 24th bodes well for socializing. There's a second Full Moon—a calendar Blue Moon—in Pisces on the 30th, making August 2023 one of the best and rarest times for several months to ignite a plan and see it through the Moon cycle to its completion.

The tarot card for August is the Devil, but this has nothing to do with demons or other nasties. This card reveals where self-made chains might be inhibiting progress. With its two Full Moons, this is the perfect month to get together a plan of action to break free, and this is supported by the secondary card for the month, the Lovers, a card representing choice. The universal month numerology number for August is 6, resonating that option for choice and encouraging you to turn your compassion and understanding toward yourself.

Aside from that amazing Blue Moon, the rest of the astrology for August is fairly quiet. On the 23rd, both the Sun and Mercury enter into Virgo. Mercury is stationing retrograde, so this is not the best time for acting on plans or starting new projects, especially as it is Virgo's ruling planet. Virgo does embrace the turtle energy, though,

and slow and steady will go a long way to reaching long-term goals; Virgo can be quite industrious! Mars goes into Libra on the 27th, which could create some frustrations and potential arguments.

September

This month opens with a waning Moon entering the fourth quarter in Gemini on the 6th, so the first week of September isn't a particularly good time for social endeavors. The New Moon in Virgo on the 14th ties in well with all the other planetary activity this month, making it a good time to scrutinize not just plans, but also relationships. The second quarter Moon in Sagittarius on the 22nd opens a favorable time for socializing and celebrating Mabon. The month closes with the Full Moon in Aries on the 29th, another fire sign and a time for plenty of energy and action.

The tarot card for September is the Tower. This may be considered to be quite an ominous card, for it does show destruction,

but it also shows the foundations are strong and brings a chance to let in the light and rebuild things even better than they were. The secondary card, the Chariot, ensures that things are moving ahead, so don't cling to what wants to evolve. Numerologically, this month is a 16 with 7 undertones. There's an undercurrent of karma here and a touch of mystery; it's important to keep egos in check at this time.

On September 4th Jupiter in Taurus stations retrograde just after Venus in Leo turns direct on the 3rd, so this could be quite a time for upheaval. Jupiter retrograde in Taurus until the end of the year has the potential to help you make great progress toward some practical goals—Taurus is an earth sign, so think turtle steps—providing laziness does not creep in. Venus direct in Leo turns on the charm, but after being held back these last few weeks, the energy might tend toward being a bit of a show-off; don't be drawn in by flashy gestures. Mercury stations direct on the 15th and brings a smoother flow to ideas and interpersonal interactions. The Sun leaves Virgo on the 23rd of September with the autumn equinox.

October

The lunar cycle for this month is very similar to September's, and reflection may bring an idea of what lies in store. The 6th sees the fourth quarter Moon in Cancer, where ties to home and family traditions might call in some way. The New Moon on the 14th in Libra could cause some people to sulk if they don't get their way—especially with the solar eclipse energy influencing things. A second quarter Moon in Capricorn will soon ground that energy, and the partial lunar eclipse of the Full Moon in Taurus on the 28th could see that energy manifest in some kind of material gain.

The tarot card for October is the Star, with additional energy brought by Strength. The Star brings hope and Strength adds integrity and endurance, making this a good month for working hard to manifest ambitions, particularly after the 19th. Numerologically,

October is a number 8, a month when hard work could be rewarded or at least recognized.

Elsewhere in the skies, Mercury enters into Libra on the 4th, which potentially improves communications. The 8th sees Venus enter into Virgo, where hard work may improve financial matters. After the 12th, Scorpio gets very busy; Mars enters the scorpion on the 12th, Mercury on the 22nd, and the Sun on the 23rd. Scorpio has a sting in the tail, so take nothing for granted while it's so packed.

November

The month opens with a fourth quarter Moon in Leo on the 5th. Sparks might fly, as Leo is a fiery sign and the waning Moon is reserved. The New Moon on the 13th in Scorpio brings a chance for introspection. On the 20th the second quarter Moon in Aquarius is a good time to look at learning something new or researching something deeper, and the month wraps up with the Full Moon in Gemini, a great time to socialize and share what has been discovered with others.

The tarot card for November is the Moon, which brings with it some uncertainty. The complimentary card is the Hermit, so should the misgivings arise, the Hermit reassures that the answers are already there, although it may take some quiet introspection to find them. In numerology, November is a universal month number 9, which matches the Hermit's introspection and brings a chance to bring things to a conclusion before the year's end.

Elsewhere in the skies, Venus enters Libra on the 8th—this is one of the signs it rules, and it's very much at home here, bringing with it a lot of charm and charisma just in time for the winter holidays. Mercury direct enters Sagittarius, bringing enamoring energy into the social mix. The 23rd sees the Sun follow Mercury into Sagittarius's fire, soon accompanied by Mars on the 24th. It all adds up to the potential for the latter half of November to be busy in a myriad of ways.

December

December's fourth quarter Moon falls in Virgo on the 4th, adding reserve and attention to details to the cosmic energy. The New Moon in Sagittarius on the 12th increases the energy for socializing and doing things on impulse. This energy increases with the waxing second quarter Moon in Pisces on the 19th, when things take a turn for the nebulous and the dreamy. The Full Moon in Cancer on the 26th increases ties to home and family, but care must be taken that moods and atmospheres don't pour cold water on activities.

The tarot card for December is the Sun, supported by the energy of both the Wheel of Fortune and the Magician, and they bring an air of optimism, change, and opportunity. The numerology universal number for this month is 1, a number of new beginnings. It emphasizes the opportunity and the potential of the tarot cards in a positive way, but there could be some confrontation.

Astrologically, Mercury enters Capricorn on the 1st, which will help stabilize plans and opportunities. Capricorn is another earth sign, with the turtle as one of its representations—and a good time to withdraw into a shell and contemplate, "What next?" The 4th sees Venus enter Scorpio, which could be challenging for finances and relationships. The winter solstice on the 22nd sees the Sun enter Capricorn, where its energy leans toward the tenacious—a good time for contemplating resolutions. The month closes with Venus entering Sagittarius on the 29th, which might not be the best time for budgets or rapport with others.

January

1 Sunday
New Year's Day • Kwanzaa ends
Waxing Moon
Moon phase: Second Quarter
Color: Orange

Moon Sign: Taurus
Incense: Almond

---

2 Monday
First Writing Day (Japanese)
Waxing Moon
Moon phase: Second Quarter
Color: White

Moon Sign: Taurus
Moon enters Gemini 9:44 pm
Incense: Lily

---

3 Tuesday
St. Genevieve's Day
Waxing Moon
Moon phase: Second Quarter
Color: Gray

Moon Sign: Gemini
Incense: Ginger

---

4 Wednesday
Kamakura Workers' Festival (Japanese)
Waxing Moon
Moon phase: Second Quarter
Color: Topaz

Moon Sign: Gemini
Incense: Lilac

---

5 Thursday
Bird Day
Waxing Moon
Moon phase: Second Quarter
Color: Crimson

Moon Sign: Gemini
Moon enters Cancer 9:15 am
Incense: Nutmeg

☺ Friday
Epiphany
Waxing Moon
Full Moon 6:08 pm
Color: Pink

Moon Sign: Cancer
Incense: Violet

---

7 Saturday
Tricolor Day (Italian)
Waning Moon
Moon phase: Third Quarter
Color: Indigo

Moon Sign: Cancer
Moon enters Leo 9:40 pm
Incense: Ivy

8 Sunday
Midwives' Day (Bulgarian)
Waning Moon
Moon phase: Third Quarter
Color: Yellow

Moon Sign: Leo
Incense: Juniper

9 Monday
Feast of the Black Nazarene (Filipino)
Waning Moon
Moon phase: Third Quarter
Color: Gray

Moon Sign: Leo
Incense: Neroli

10 Tuesday
Feast of St. Leonie Aviat
Waning Moon
Moon phase: Third Quarter
Color: Maroon

Moon Sign: Leo
Moon enters Virgo 10:15 am
Incense: Cinnamon

11 Wednesday
Carmentalia (Roman)
Waning Moon
Moon phase: Third Quarter
Color: Brown

Moon Sign: Virgo
Incense: Marjoram

12 Thursday
Revolution Day (Tanzanian)
Waning Moon
Moon phase: Third Quarter
Color: Turquoise

Moon Sign: Virgo
Moon enters Libra 9:56 pm
Incense: Apricot

13 Friday
Vogel Gryff (Swiss)
Waning Moon
Moon phase: Third Quarter
Color: Purple

Moon Sign: Libra
Incense: Alder

☽ Saturday
Feast of the Ass (French)
Waning Moon
Fourth Quarter 9:10 pm
Color: Blue

Moon Sign: Libra
Incense: Patchouli

January

15 Sunday
Korean Alphabet Day
Waning Moon
Moon phase: Fourth Quarter
Color: Amber

Moon Sign: Libra
Moon enters Scorpio 7:08 am
Incense: Eucalyptus

16 Monday
Martin Luther King Jr. Day
Waning Moon
Moon phase: Fourth Quarter
Color: Silver

Moon Sign: Scorpio
Incense: Clary sage

17 Tuesday
St. Anthony's Day (Mexican)
Waning Moon
Moon phase: Fourth Quarter
Color: Black

Moon Sign: Scorpio
Moon enters Sagittarius 12:33 pm
Incense: Bayberry

18 Wednesday
Feast of St. Athanasius
Waning Moon
Moon phase: Fourth Quarter
Color: White

Moon Sign: Sagittarius
Incense: Lavender

19 Thursday
Edgar Allan Poe's birthday
Waning Moon
Moon phase: Fourth Quarter
Color: Purple

Moon Sign: Sagittarius
Moon enters Capricorn 2:11 pm
Incense: Mulberry

20 Friday
Husband's Day (Icelandic)
Waning Moon
Moon phase: Fourth Quarter
Color: Coral

Moon Sign: Capricorn
Sun enters Aquarius 3:30 am
Incense: Mint

Saturday
St. Agnes's Day
Waning Moon
New Moon 3:53 pm
Color: Brown

Moon Sign: Capricorn
Moon enters Aquarius 1:29 pm
Incense: Sage

January

22 Sunday
Lunar New Year (Rabbit)
Waxing Moon
Moon phase: First Quarter
Color: Gold

Moon Sign: Aquarius
Incense: Heliotrope

23 Monday
Feast of St. Ildefonsus
Waxing Moon
Moon phase: First Quarter
Color: Lavender

Moon Sign: Aquarius
Moon enters Pisces 12:36 pm
Incense: Rosemary

24 Tuesday
Alasitas Fair (Bolivian)
Waxing Moon
Moon phase: First Quarter
Color: Scarlet

Moon Sign: Pisces
Incense: Geranium

25 Wednesday
Burns Night (Scottish)
Waxing Moon
Moon phase: First Quarter
Color: Yellow

Moon Sign: Pisces
Moon enters Aries 1:48 pm
Incense: Bay laurel

26 Thursday
Australia Day
Waxing Moon
Moon phase: First Quarter
Color: Green

Moon Sign: Aries
Myrrh

27 Friday
Holocaust Remembrance Day
Waxing Moon
Moon phase: First Quarter
Color: White

Moon Sign: Aries
Moon enters Taurus 6:42 pm
Incense: Vanilla

☾ Saturday
St. Charlemagne's Day
Waxing Moon
Second Quarter 10:19 am
Color: Black

Moon Sign: Taurus
Incense: Rue

January

29 Sunday
Feast of St. Gildas
Waxing Moon
Moon phase: Second Quarter
Color: Orange

Moon Sign: Taurus
Incense: Frankincense

30 Monday
Gasparilla Pirate Festival (Floridian)
Waxing Moon
Moon phase: Second Quarter
Color: Ivory

Moon Sign: Taurus
Moon enters Gemini 3:35 am
Incense: Narcissus

31 Tuesday
Independence Day (Nauru)
Waxing Moon
Moon phase: Second Quarter
Color: Red

Moon Sign: Gemini
Incense: Cedar

January Correspondences

Stones: Garnet, moonstone
Animals: Snow goose, owl, bear, wolf
Flowers: Carnation, snowdrop
Deities: Baba Yaga, Enki, Hekate, Loki, Saturn
Zodiac: Capricorn

February Correspondences

Stones: Amethyst, obsidian
Animals: Otter, white cow, snake
Flowers: Violet, primrose
Deities: Brigid, Ea, Ishtar, Isis, Juno, Nut
Zodiac: Aquarius

February

1 Wednesday
St. Brigid's Day (Irish)
Waxing Moon
Moon phase: Second Quarter
Color: Topaz

Moon Sign: Gemini
Moon enters Cancer 3:11 pm
Incense: Honeysuckle

---

2 Thursday
Imbolc • Groundhog Day
Waxing Moon
Moon phase: Second Quarter
Color: White

Moon Sign: Cancer
Incense: Carnation

---

3 Friday
St. Blaise's Day
Waxing Moon
Moon phase: Second Quarter
Color: Rose

Moon Sign: Cancer
Incense: Orchid

---

4 Saturday
Independence Day (Sri Lankan)
Waxing Moon
Moon phase: Second Quarter
Color: Gray

Moon Sign: Cancer
Moon enters Leo 3:48 am
Incense: Magnolia

---

5 Sunday
Lantern Festival (Chinese)
Waxing Moon
Full Moon 1:29 pm
Color: Gold

Moon Sign: Leo
Incense: Hyacinth

---

6 Monday
Bob Marley's birthday (Jamaican)
Waning Moon
Moon phase: Third Quarter
Color: White

Moon Sign: Leo
Moon enters Virgo 4:14 pm
Incense: Hyssop

---

7 Tuesday
Feast of St. Richard the Pilgrim
Waning Moon
Moon phase: Third Quarter
Color: Black

Moon Sign: Virgo
Incense: Basil

8 Wednesday

Prešeren Day (Slovenian)
Waning Moon
Moon phase: Third Quarter
Color: Yellow

Moon Sign: Virgo
Incense: Lilac

9 Thursday

St. Maron's Day (Lebanese)
Waning Moon
Moon phase: Third Quarter
Color: Green

Moon Sign: Virgo
Moon enters Libra 3:47 am
Incense: Balsam

10 Friday

Feast of St. Scholastica
Waning Moon
Moon phase: Third Quarter
Color: Pink

Moon Sign: Libra
Incense: Rose

11 Saturday

National Foundation Day (Japanese)
Waning Moon
Moon phase: Third Quarter
Color: Brown

Moon Sign: Libra
Moon enters Scorpio 1:34 pm
Incense: Sandalwood

12 Sunday

Revolution Day (Tanzanian)
Waning Moon
Moon phase: Third Quarter
Color: Orange

Moon Sign: Scorpio
Incense: Marigold

☾ Monday

Parentalia
Waning Moon
Fourth Quarter 11:01 am
Color: Ivory

Moon Sign: Scorpio
Moon enters Sagittarius 8:31 pm
Incense: Lily

14 Tuesday

Valentine's Day
Waning Moon
Moon phase: Fourth Quarter
Color: Maroon

Moon Sign: Sagittarius
Incense: Ylang-ylang

15 Wednesday

Susan B. Anthony Day
Waning Moon
Moon phase: Fourth Quarter
Color: White

Moon Sign: Sagittarius
Incense: Bay laurel

16 Thursday

Nichiren's birthday
Waning Moon
Moon phase: Fourth Quarter
Color: Crimson

Moon Sign: Sagittarius
Moon enters Capricorn 12:00 am
Incense: Jasmine

17 Friday

Quirinalia (Roman)
Waning Moon
Moon phase: Fourth Quarter
Color: Purple

Moon Sign: Capricorn
Incense: Vanilla

18 Saturday

St. Bernadette's Third Vision
Waning Moon
Moon phase: Fourth Quarter
Color: Blue

Moon Sign: Capricorn
Sun enters Pisces 5:34 pm
Moon enters Aquarius 12:35 am
Incense: Pine

19 Sunday

Flag Day (Turkmenian)
Waning Moon
Moon phase: Fourth Quarter
Color: Yellow

Moon Sign: Aquarius
Moon enters Pisces 11:56 pm
Incense: Juniper

Monday

Presidents' Day
Waning Moon
New Moon 2:06 am
Color: Lavender

Moon Sign: Pisces
Incense: Rosemary

21 Tuesday

Mardi Gras (Fat Tuesday)
Waxing Moon
Moon phase: First Quarter
Color: Red

Moon Sign: Pisces
Incense: Ginger

February

22 Wednesday
Ash Wednesday
Waxing Moon
Moon phase: First Quarter
Color: Brown

Moon Sign: Pisces
Moon enters Aries 12:14 am
Incense: Marjoram

---

23 Thursday
Mashramani Festival (Guyanan)
Waxing Moon
Moon phase: First Quarter
Color: Turquoise

Moon Sign: Aries
Incense: Clove

---

24 Friday
Regifugium (Roman)
Waxing Moon
Moon phase: First Quarter
Color: Coral

Moon Sign: Aries
Moon enters Taurus 3:29 am
Incense: Yarrow

---

25 Saturday
St. Walburga's Day (German)
Waxing Moon
Moon phase: First Quarter
Color: Black

Moon Sign: Taurus
Incense: Sage

---

26 Sunday
Zamboanga Day (Filipino)
Waxing Moon
Moon phase: First Quarter
Color: Amber

Moon Sign: Taurus
Moon enters Gemini 10:48 am
Incense: Almond

☾ Monday
Independence Day (Dominican)
Waxing Moon
Second Quarter 3:06 am
Color: Gray

Moon Sign: Gemini
Incense: Neroli

---

28 Tuesday
Kalevala Day (Finnish)
Waxing Moon
Moon phase: Second Quarter
Color: White

Moon Sign: Gemini
Moon enters Cancer 9:40 pm
Incense: Cedar

March

1 **Wednesday**
Matronalia (Roman)
Waxing Moon
Moon phase: Second Quarter
Color: Yellow

Moon Sign: Cancer
Incense: Honeysuckle

---

2 **Thursday**
Read Across America Day
Waxing Moon
Moon phase: Second Quarter
Color: Green

Moon Sign: Cancer
Incense: Nutmeg

---

3 **Friday**
Doll Festival (Japanese)
Waxing Moon
Moon phase: Second Quarter
Color: Rose

Moon Sign: Cancer
Moon enters Leo 10:16 am
Incense: Thyme

---

4 **Saturday**
St. Casimir's Fair (Lithuanian and Polish)
Waxing Moon
Moon phase: Second Quarter
Color: Indigo

Moon Sign: Leo
Incense: Sandalwood

---

5 **Sunday**
Navigium Isidis Festival (Roman)
Waxing Moon
Moon phase: Second Quarter
Color: Yellow

Moon Sign: Leo
Moon enters Virgo 10:38 pm
Incense: Marigold

---

6 **Monday**
Purim begins at sundown
Waxing Moon
Moon phase: Second Quarter
Color: Silver

Moon Sign: Virgo
Incense: Narcissus

☺ **Tuesday**
Vejovis Festival (Roman)
Waxing Moon
Full Moon 7:40 am
Color: Scarlet

Moon Sign: Virgo
Incense: Cinnamon

March

8 Wednesday
International Women's Day
Waning Moon
Moon phase: Third Quarter
Color: Topaz

Moon Sign: Virgo
Moon enters Libra 9:44 am
Incense: Lavender

---

9 Thursday
Teachers' Day (Lebanese)
Waning Moon
Moon phase: Third Quarter
Color: White

Moon Sign: Libra
Incense: Clove

---

10 Friday
Tibet Uprising Day
Waning Moon
Moon phase: Third Quarter
Color: Purple

Moon Sign: Libra
Moon enters Scorpio 7:06 pm
Incense: Cypress

---

11 Saturday
National Foundation Day (Japanese)
Waning Moon
Moon phase: Third Quarter
Color: Blue

Moon Sign: Scorpio
Incense: Patchouli

---

12 Sunday
Girl Scouts' birthday
Waning Moon
Moon phase: Third Quarter
Color: Gold

Moon Sign: Scorpio
Incense: Hyacinth

Daylight Saving Time begins at 2 am

---

13 Monday
Feast of St. Leander of Seville
Waning Moon
Moon phase: Third Quarter
Color: Lavender

Moon Sign: Scorpio
Moon enters Sagittarius 3:21 am
Incense: Clary sage

○ Tuesday
Pi Day
Waning Moon
Fourth Quarter 10:08 pm
Color: Gray

Moon Sign: Sagittarius
Incense: Basil

March

15 Wednesday
Fertility Festival (Japanese)
Waning Moon
Moon phase: Fourth Quarter
Color: Brown

Moon Sign: Sagittarius
Moon enters Capricorn 8:06 am
Incense: Lilac

---

16 Thursday
Oranges and Lemons Service (English)
Waning Moon
Moon phase: Fourth Quarter
Color: Crimson

Moon Sign: Capricorn
Incense: Myrrh

---

17 Friday
St. Patrick's Day
Waning Moon
Moon phase: Fourth Quarter
Color: Coral

Moon Sign: Capricorn
Moon enters Aquarius 10:25 am
Incense: Alder

---

18 Saturday
Sheila's Day (Irish)
Waning Moon
Moon phase: Fourth Quarter
Color: Black

Moon Sign: Aquarius
Incense: Magnolia

---

19 Sunday
Minna Canth's birthday (Finnish)
Waning Moon
Moon phase: Fourth Quarter
Color: Orange

Moon Sign: Aquarius
Moon enters Pisces 11:12 am
Incense: Frankincense

---

20 Monday
Ostara • Spring Equinox
Waning Moon
Moon phase: Fourth Quarter
Color: Ivory

Moon Sign: Pisces
Sun enters Aries 5:24 pm
Incense: Hyssop

🌑 Tuesday
Juarez Day (Mexican)
Waning Moon
New Moon 1:23 pm
Color: Red

Moon Sign: Pisces
Moon enters Aries 12:01 pm
Incense: Bayberry

March

22 Wednesday
Ramadan begins at sundown
Waxing Moon
Moon phase: First Quarter
Color: Yellow

Moon Sign: Aries
Incense: Bay laurel

---

23 Thursday
Pakistan Day
Waxing Moon
Moon phase: First Quarter
Color: Purple

Moon Sign: Aries
Moon enters Taurus 2:42 pm
Incense: Jasmine

---

24 Friday
Day of Blood (Roman)
Waxing Moon
Moon phase: First Quarter
Color: White

Moon Sign: Taurus
Incense: Orchid

---

25 Saturday
Tolkien Reading Day
Waxing Moon
Moon phase: First Quarter
Color: Gray

Moon Sign: Taurus
Moon enters Gemini 8:42 pm
Incense: Ivy

---

26 Sunday
Prince Kuhio Day (Hawaiian)
Waxing Moon
Moon phase: First Quarter
Color: Yellow

Moon Sign: Gemini
Incense: Heliotrope

---

27 Monday
Passover begins at sundown
Waxing Moon
Moon phase: First Quarter
Color: White

Moon Sign: Gemini
Incense: Lily

◐ **Tuesday**
Weed Appreciation Day
Waxing Moon
Second Quarter 10:32 pm
Color: Maroon

Moon Sign: Gemini
Moon enters Cancer 6:22 am
Incense: Ylang-ylang

29 Wednesday

Feast of St. Eustace of Luxeuil
Waxing Moon
Moon phase: Second Quarter
Color: Brown

Moon Sign: Cancer
Incense: Marjoram

---

30 Thursday

Seward's Day (Alaskan)
Waxing Moon
Moon phase: Second Quarter
Color: Turquoise

Moon Sign: Cancer
Moon enters Leo 6:31 pm
Incense: Mulberry

---

31 Friday

César Chávez Day
Waxing Moon
Moon phase: Second Quarter
Color: Pink

Moon Sign: Leo
Incense: Yarrow

March Correspondences

Stones: Aquamarine, jade, bloodstone, jasper
Animals: Cougar, whale, rabbit, frog
Flowers: Daffodil, narcissus
Deities: Diana, Kwan Yin, Poseidon, Sedna, Yemaya
Zodiac: Pisces

April

1 Saturday
All Fools' Day • April Fools' Day
Waxing Moon
Moon phase: Second Quarter
Color: Blue

Moon Sign: Leo
Incense: Rue

---

2 Sunday
Palm Sunday
Waxing Moon
Moon phase: Second Quarter
Color: Gold

Moon Sign: Leo
Moon enters Virgo 6:57 am
Incense: Eucalyptus

---

3 Monday
Feast of St. Mary of Egypt
Waxing Moon
Moon phase: Second Quarter
Color: Gray

Moon Sign: Virgo
Incense: Clary sage

---

4 Tuesday
Megalesia (Roman)
Waxing Moon
Moon phase: Second Quarter
Color: Black

Moon Sign: Virgo
Moon enters Libra 5:51 pm
Incense: Geranium

---

5 Wednesday
Passover begins at sundown
Waxing Moon
Moon phase: Second Quarter
Color: White

Moon Sign: Libra
Incense: Lavender

---

6 Thursday
Tartan Day
Waxing Moon
Full Moon 12:34 am
Color: Crimson

Moon Sign: Libra
Incense: Balsam

---

7 Friday
Good Friday
Waning Moon
Moon phase: Third Quarter
Color: Purple

Moon Sign: Libra
Moon enters Scorpio 2:29 am
Incense: Mint

8 **Saturday**
Buddha's birthday
Waning Moon
Moon phase: Third Quarter
Color: Brown

Moon Sign: Scorpio
Incense: Pine

---

9 **Sunday**
Easter
Waning Moon
Moon phase: Third Quarter
Color: Amber

Moon Sign: Scorpio
Moon enters Sagittarius 8:57 am
Incense: Almond

---

10 **Monday**
Siblings Day
Waning Moon
Moon phase: Third Quarter
Color: Silver

Moon Sign: Sagittarius
Incense: Neroli

---

11 **Tuesday**
Juan Santamaría Day (Costa Rican)
Waning Moon
Moon phase: Third Quarter
Color: Gray

Moon Sign: Sagittarius
Moon enters Capricorn 1:33 pm
Incense: Ginger

---

12 **Wednesday**
Children's Day (Bolivian and Haitian)
Waning Moon
Moon phase: Third Quarter
Color: Topaz

Moon Sign: Capricorn
Incense: Marjoram

☽ Thursday
Passover ends
Waning Moon
Fourth Quarter 5:11 am
Color: Green

Moon Sign: Capricorn
Moon enters Aquarius 4:42 pm
Incense: Apricot

---

14 **Friday**
Orthodox Good Friday
Waning Moon
Moon phase: Fourth Quarter
Color: Coral

Moon Sign: Aquarius
Incense: Rose

April

15 Saturday

Fordicidia (Roman)
Waning Moon
Moon phase: Fourth Quarter
Color: Indigo

Moon Sign: Aquarius
Moon enters Pisces 6:57 pm
Incense: Ivy

16 Sunday

Orthodox Easter
Waning Moon
Moon phase: Fourth Quarter
Color: Yellow

Moon Sign: Pisces
Incense: Heliotrope

17 Monday

Sechseläuten (Swiss)
Waning Moon
Moon phase: Fourth Quarter
Color: Ivory

Moon Sign: Pisces
Moon enters Aries 9:09 pm
Incense: Hyssop

18 Tuesday

International Day for Monuments and Sites
Waning Moon
Moon phase: Fourth Quarter
Color: Red

Moon Sign: Aries
Incense: Ylang-ylang

19 Wednesday

Primrose Day (British)
Waning Moon
Moon phase: Fourth Quarter
Color: Brown

Moon Sign: Aries
Incense: Lilac

☽ Thursday

Drum Festival (Japanese)
Waning Moon
New Moon 12:13 am
Color: Turquoise

Moon Sign: Aries
Moon enters Taurus 12:30 am
Sun enters Taurus 4:14 am
Incense: Carnation

21 Friday

Ramadan ends
Waxing Moon
Moon phase: First Quarter
Color: Rose

Moon Sign: Taurus
Incense: Thyme

April

22 Saturday
Earth Day
Waxing Moon
Moon phase: First Quarter
Color: Blue

Moon Sign: Taurus
Moon enters Gemini 6:11 am
Incense: Patchouli

23 Sunday
St. George's Day (English)
Waxing Moon
Moon phase: First Quarter
Color: Orange

Moon Sign: Gemini
Incense: Marigold

24 Monday
St. Mark's Eve
Waxing Moon
Moon phase: First Quarter
Color: Gray

Moon Sign: Gemini
Moon enters Cancer 2:58 pm
Incense: Narcissus

25 Tuesday
Robigalia (Roman)
Waxing Moon
Moon phase: First Quarter
Color: Scarlet

Moon Sign: Cancer
Incense: Basil

26 Wednesday
Chernobyl Remembrance Day (Belarusian)
Waxing Moon
Moon phase: First Quarter
Color: Topaz

Moon Sign: Cancer
Incense: Honeysuckle

☽ Thursday
Freedom Day (South African)
Waxing Moon
Second Quarter 5:20 pm
Color: White

Moon Sign: Cancer
Moon enters Leo 2:30 am
Incense: Nutmeg

28 Friday
Floralia (Roman) • Arbor Day
Waxing Moon
Moon phase: Second Quarter
Color: Purple

Moon Sign: Leo
Incense: Violet

29 Saturday

Showa Day (Japanese)
Waxing Moon
Moon phase: Second Quarter
Color: Black

Moon Sign: Leo
Moon enters Virgo 2:59 pm
Incense: Sage

---

30 Sunday

Walpurgis Night
Waxing Moon
Moon phase: Second Quarter
Color: Amber

Moon Sign: Virgo
Incense: Eucalyptus

April Correspondences

Stones: Beryl, diamond, moonstone
Animals: Falcon, hawk, goat, sheep
Flowers: Sweet pea, daisy
Deities: Ares, Macha, the Morrigan, Ra
Zodiac: Aries

May

1 Monday
Beltane
Waxing Moon
Moon phase: Second Quarter
Color: White

Moon Sign: Virgo
Incense: Rosemary

2 Tuesday
Teacher Appreciation Day
Waxing Moon
Moon phase: Second Quarter
Color: Maroon

Moon Sign: Virgo
Moon enters Libra 2:09 am
Incense: Cedar

3 Wednesday
Roodmas
Waxing Moon
Moon phase: Second Quarter
Color: Yellow

Moon Sign: Libra
Incense: Bay laurel

4 Thursday
Star Wars Day
Waxing Moon
Moon phase: Second Quarter
Color: Purple

Moon Sign: Libra
Moon enters Scorpio 10:32 am
Incense: Balsam

☺ Friday
Cinco de Mayo (Mexican)
Waxing Moon
Full Moon 1:34 pm
Color: Rose

Moon Sign: Scorpio
Incense: Vanilla

6 Saturday
Martyrs' Day (Lebanese and Syrian)
Waning Moon
Moon phase: Third Quarter
Color: Blue

Moon Sign: Scorpio
Moon enters Sagittarius 4:04 pm
Incense: Rue

7 Sunday
Pilgrimage of St. Nicholas (Italian)
Waning Moon
Moon phase: Third Quarter
Color: Gold

Moon Sign: Sagittarius
Incense: Hyacinth

May

8 **Monday**
White Lotus Day (Theosophical)
Waning Moon
Moon phase: Third Quarter
Color: Lavender

Moon Sign: Sagittarius
Moon enters Capricorn 7:33 pm
Incense: Hyssop

9 **Tuesday**
Lemuria (Roman)
Waning Moon
Moon phase: Third Quarter
Color: Red

Moon Sign: Capricorn
Incense: Geranium

10 **Wednesday**
Independence Day (Romanian)
Waning Moon
Moon phase: Third Quarter
Color: White

Moon Sign: Capricorn
Moon enters Aquarius 10:05 pm
Incense: Lavender

11 **Thursday**
Ukai season opens (Japanese)
Waning Moon
Moon phase: Third Quarter
Color: Turquoise

Moon Sign: Aquarius
Incense: Myrrh

☾ **Friday**
Florence Nightingale's birthday
Waning Moon
Fourth Quarter 10:28 am
Color: White

Moon Sign: Aquarius
Incense: Thyme

13 **Saturday**
Pilgrimage to Fátima (Portuguese)
Waning Moon
Moon phase: Fourth Quarter
Color: Indigo

Moon Sign: Aquarius
Moon enters Pisces 12:39 am
Incense: Magnolia

14 **Sunday**
Mother's Day
Waning Moon
Moon phase: Fourth Quarter
Color: Yellow

Moon Sign: Pisces
Incense: Juniper

15 **Monday**
Festival of St. Dymphna
Waning Moon
Moon phase: Fourth Quarter
Color: Silver

Moon Sign: Pisces
Moon enters Aries 3:56 am
Incense: Narcissus

---

16 **Tuesday**
St. Honoratus's Day
Waning Moon
Moon phase: Fourth Quarter
Color: Scarlet

Moon Sign: Aries
Incense: Bayberry

---

17 **Wednesday**
Norwegian Constitution Day
Waning Moon
Moon phase: Fourth Quarter
Color: Brown

Moon Sign: Aries
Moon enters Taurus 8:28 am
Incense: Marjoram

---

18 **Thursday**
Battle of Las Piedras Day (Uruguayan)
Waning Moon
Moon phase: Fourth Quarter
Color: Green

Moon Sign: Taurus
Incense: Carnation

Friday
Mother's Day (Kyrgyzstani)
Waning Moon
New Moon 11:53 am
Color: Pink

Moon Sign: Taurus
Moon enters Gemini 2:48 pm
Incense: Yarrow

---

20 **Saturday**
Feast of St. Aurea of Ostia
Waxing Moon
Moon phase: First Quarter
Color: Gray

Moon Sign: Gemini
Sun enters Gemini 3:09 am
Incense: Sandalwood

---

21 **Sunday**
Navy Day (Chilean)
Waxing Moon
Moon phase: First Quarter
Color: Gold

Moon Sign: Gemini
Moon enters Cancer 11:28 pm
Incense: Frankincense

May

22 Monday
Victoria Day (Canadian)
Waxing Moon
Moon phase: First Quarter
Color: Gray

Moon Sign: Cancer
Incense: Clary sage

23 Tuesday
Tubilustrium (Roman)
Waxing Moon
Moon phase: First Quarter
Color: Maroon

Moon Sign: Cancer
Incense: Cinnamon

24 Wednesday
Education and Culture Day (Bulgaria)
Waxing Moon
Moon phase: First Quarter
Color: Topaz

Moon Sign: Cancer
Moon enters Leo 10:35 am
Incense: Lilac

25 Thursday
Shavuot begins at sundown
Waxing Moon
Moon phase: First Quarter
Color: Crimson

Moon Sign: Leo
Incense: Mulberry

26 Friday
Pepys's Commemoration (English)
Waxing Moon
Moon phase: First Quarter
Color: Coral

Moon Sign: Leo
Moon enters Virgo 11:05 pm
Incense: Cypress

◑ Saturday
Feast of St. Bede the Venerable
Waxing Moon
Second Quarter 11:22 am
Color: Brown

Moon Sign: Virgo
Incense: Sage

28 Sunday
St. Germain's Day
Waxing Moon
Moon phase: Second Quarter
Color: Orange

Moon Sign: Virgo
Incense: Marigold

May

29 Monday
Memorial Day
Waxing Moon
Moon phase: Second Quarter
Color: Ivory

Moon Sign: Virgo
Moon enters Libra 10:51 am
Incense: Lily

---

30 Tuesday
Canary Islands Day
Waxing Moon
Moon phase: Second Quarter
Color: Black

Moon Sign: Libra
Incense: Ginger

---

31 Wednesday
Visitation of Mary
Waxing Moon
Moon phase: Second Quarter
Color: Yellow

Moon Sign: Libra
Moon enters Scorpio 7:45 pm
Incense: Honeysuckle

May Correspondences

Stones: Agate, emerald, carnelian
Animals: Beaver, cow, elk
Flower: Lily of the valley
Deities: Aphrodite, Dionysus, Gaia, Horus, Osiris
Zodiac: Taurus

June

1   Wednesday
Dayak Harvest Festival (Malaysian)
Waxing Moon
Moon phase: Second Quarter
Color: Green

Moon Sign: Scorpio
Incense: Clove

---

2   Friday
Republic Day (Italian)
Waxing Moon
Moon phase: Second Quarter
Color: Pink

Moon Sign: Scorpio
Incense: Thyme

☺   Saturday
Feast of St. Clotilde
Waxing Moon
Full Moon 11:42 pm
Color: Indigo

Moon Sign: Scorpio
Moon enters Sagittarius 1:03 am
Incense: Magnolia

---

4   Sunday
Flag Day (Estonian)
Waning Moon
Moon phase: Third Quarter
Color: Orange

Moon Sign: Sagittarius
Incense: Juniper

---

5   Monday
Constitution Day (Danish)
Waning Moon
Moon phase: Third Quarter
Color: Lavender

Moon Sign: Sagittarius
Moon enters Capricorn 3:31 am
Incense: Hyssop

---

6   Tuesday
National Day of Sweden
Waning Moon
Moon phase: Third Quarter
Color: White

Moon Sign: Capricorn
Incense: Basil

---

7   Wednesday
Vestalia begins (Roman)
Waning Moon
Moon phase: Third Quarter
Color: Brown

Moon Sign: Capricorn
Moon enters Aquarius 4:42 am
Incense: Marjoram

June

8 Thursday
World Oceans Day
Waning Moon
Moon phase: Third Quarter
Color: Purple

Moon Sign: Aquarius
Incense: Apricot

9 Friday
Heroes' Day (Ugandan)
Waning Moon
Moon phase: Third Quarter
Color: Rose

Moon Sign: Aquarius
Moon enters Pisces 6:14 am
Incense: Orchid

☽ Saturday
Portugal Day
Waning Moon
Fourth Quarter 3:31 pm
Color: Gray

Moon Sign: Pisces
Incense: Ivy

11 Sunday
Kamehameha Day (Hawaiian)
Waning Moon
Moon phase: Fourth Quarter
Color: Yellow

Moon Sign: Pisces
Moon enters Aries 9:20 am
Incense: Heliotrope

12 Monday
Independence Day (Filipino)
Waning Moon
Moon phase: Fourth Quarter
Color: White

Moon Sign: Aries
Incense: Rosemary

13 Tuesday
St. Anthony of Padua's Day
Waning Moon
Moon phase: Fourth Quarter
Color: Red

Moon Sign: Aries
Moon enters Taurus 2:31 pm
Incense: Geranium

14 Wednesday
Flag Day
Waning Moon
Moon phase: Fourth Quarter
Color: Topaz

Moon Sign: Taurus
Incense: Honeysuckle

June

15 Thursday
Vestalia ends (Roman)
Waning Moon
Moon phase: Fourth Quarter
Color: Crimson

Moon Sign: Taurus
Moon enters Gemini 9:46 pm
Incense: Jasmine

16 Friday
Bloomsday (Irish)
Waning Moon
Moon phase: Fourth Quarter
Color: Coral

Moon Sign: Gemini
Incense: Vanilla

17 Saturday
Bunker Hill Day (Massachusetts)
Waning Moon
Moon phase: Fourth Quarter
Color: Blue

Moon Sign: Gemini
Incense: Rue

Sunday
Father's Day
Waning Moon
New Moon 12:37 am
Color: Amber

Moon Sign: Gemini
Moon enters Cancer 6:58 am
Incense: Hyacinth

19 Monday
Juneteenth
Waxing Moon
Moon phase: First Quarter
Color: Gray

Moon Sign: Cancer
Incense: Neroli

20 Tuesday
Flag Day (Argentinian)
Waxing Moon
Moon phase: First Quarter
Color: Maroon

Moon Sign: Cancer
Moon enters Leo 6:04 pm
Incense: Cinnamon

21 Wednesday
Litha • Summer Solstice
Waxing Moon
Moon phase: First Quarter
Color: Brown

Moon Sign: Leo
Sun enters Cancer 10:58 am
Incense: Lavender

June

22 Thursday
Teachers' Day (El Salvadoran)
Waxing Moon
Moon phase: First Quarter
Color: Turquoise

Moon Sign: Leo
Incense: Nutmeg

23 Friday
St. John's Eve
Waxing Moon
Moon phase: First Quarter
Color: Purple

Moon Sign: Leo
Moon enters Virgo 6:35 am
Incense: Rose

24 Saturday
St. John's Day
Waxing Moon
Moon phase: First Quarter
Color: Indigo

Moon Sign: Virgo
Incense: Sage

25 Sunday
Fiesta de Santa Orosia (Spanish)
Waxing Moon
Moon phase: First Quarter
Color: Gold

Moon Sign: Virgo
Moon enters Libra 6:57 pm
Incense: Almond

☾ Monday
Pied Piper Day (German)
Waxing Moon
Second Quarter 3:50 am
Color: Silver

Moon Sign: Libra
Incense: Narcissus

27 Tuesday
Seven Sleepers' Day (German)
Waxing Moon
Moon phase: Second Quarter
Color: Black

Moon Sign: Libra
Incense: Ylang-ylang

28 Wednesday
Christopher Street Day (German & Swiss)
Waxing Moon
Moon phase: Second Quarter
Color: Yellow

Moon Sign: Libra
Moon enters Scorpio 4:55 am
Incense: Lilac

June

29 Thursday

Haro Wine Battle (Spanish)
Waxing Moon
Moon phase: Second Quarter
Color: White

Moon Sign: Scorpio
Incense: Myrrh

---

30 Friday

The Burning of the Three Firs (French)
Waxing Moon
Moon phase: Second Quarter
Color: Rose

Moon Sign: Scorpio
Moon enters Sagittarius 10:59 am
Incense: Alder

June Correspondences

Stones: Pearl, chalcedony, alexandrite
Animals: Deer, eagle, fox
Flower: Rose
Deities: Artemis, Cerridwen, Hermes, Odin
Zodiac: Gemini

July

1 Saturday
Canada Day • Tartan Day (Australian)
Waxing Moon
Moon phase: Second Quarter
Color: Blue

Moon Sign: Sagittarius
Incense: Sandalwood

2 Sunday
World UFO Day
Waxing Moon
Moon phase: Second Quarter
Color: Yellow

Moon Sign: Sagittarius
Moon enters Capricorn 1:20 pm
Incense: Eucalyptus

☺ Monday
Dog Days of Summer begin
Waxing Moon
Full Moon 7:39 am
Color: Gray

Moon Sign: Capricorn
Incense: Clary sage

4 Tuesday
Independence Day
Waning Moon
Moon phase: Third Quarter
Color: Scarlet

Moon Sign: Capricorn
Moon enters Aquarius 1:30 pm
Incense: Cedar

5 Wednesday
Tynwald Day (Manx)
Waning Moon
Moon phase: Third Quarter
Color: Topaz

Moon Sign: Aquarius
Incense: Bay laurel

6 Thursday
San Fermín begins (Spanish)
Waning Moon
Moon phase: Third Quarter
Color: Green

Moon Sign: Aquarius
Moon enters Pisces 1:33 pm
Incense: Mulberry

7 Friday
Star Festival (Japanese)
Waning Moon
Moon phase: Third Quarter
Color: Purple

Moon Sign: Pisces
Incense: Violet

July

8 **Saturday**
Feast of St. Sunniva
Waning Moon
Moon phase: Third Quarter
Color: Black

Moon Sign: Pisces
Moon enters Aries 3:19 pm
Incense: Patchouli

Sunday
Battle of Sempach Day (Swiss)
Waning Moon
Fourth Quarter 9:48 pm
Color: Gold

Moon Sign: Aries
Incense: Juniper

10 **Monday**
Nicola Tesla Day
Waning Moon
Moon phase: Fourth Quarter
Color: White

Moon Sign: Aries
Moon enters Taurus 7:55 pm
Incense: Lily

11 **Tuesday**
Mongolian Naadam Festival (ends July 13)
Waning Moon
Moon phase: Fourth Quarter
Color: Gray

Moon Sign: Taurus
Incense: Bayberry

12 **Wednesday**
Malala Day
Waning Moon
Moon phase: Fourth Quarter
Color: Yellow

Moon Sign: Taurus
Incense: Marjoram

13 **Thursday**
Feast of St. Mildrith
Waning Moon
Moon phase: Fourth Quarter
Color: Turquoise

Moon Sign: Taurus
Moon enters Gemini 3:26 am
Incense: Apricot

14 **Friday**
Bastille Day (French)
Waning Moon
Moon phase: Fourth Quarter
Color: Pink

Moon Sign: Gemini
Incense: Orchid

July

15 Saturday

St. Swithin's Day
Waning Moon
Moon phase: Fourth Quarter
Color: Indigo

Moon Sign: Gemini
Moon enters Cancer 1:13 pm
Incense: Ivy

16 Sunday

Fiesta de la Tirana (Chilean)
Waning Moon
Moon phase: Fourth Quarter
Color: Amber

Moon Sign: Cancer
Incense: Hyacinth

☽ Monday

Luis Muñoz Rivera Day (Puerto Rican)
Waning Moon
New Moon 2:32 pm
Color: Ivory

Moon Sign: Cancer
Incense: Neroli

18 Tuesday

Islamic New Year begins at sundown
Waxing Moon
Moon phase: First Quarter
Color: Red

Moon Sign: Cancer
Moon enters Leo 12:39 am
Incense: Ginger

19 Wednesday

Flitch Day (English)
Waxing Moon
Moon phase: First Quarter
Color: White

Moon Sign: Leo
Incense: Lavender

20 Thursday

Binding of Wreaths (Lithuanian)
Waxing Moon
Moon phase: First Quarter
Color: Purple

Moon Sign: Leo
Moon enters Virgo 1:13 pm
Incense: Clove

21 Friday

National Day (Belgian)
Waxing Moon
Moon phase: First Quarter
Color: Coral

Moon Sign: Virgo
Incense: Yarrow

July

22 Saturday
St. Mary Magdalene's Day
Waxing Moon
Moon phase: First Quarter
Color: Gray

Moon Sign: Virgo
Sun enters Leo 9:50 pm
Incense: Pine

23 Sunday
Mysteries of St. Cristina (Italian)
Waxing Moon
Moon phase: First Quarter
Color: Orange

Moon Sign: Virgo
Moon enters Libra 1:54 am
Incense: Marigold

24 Monday
Gion Festival second Yamaboko parade (Japanese)
Waxing Moon
Moon phase: First Quarter
Color: Lavender

Moon Sign: Libra
Incense: Hyssop

◐ Tuesday
Illapa Festival (Incan)
Waxing Moon
Second Quarter 6:07 pm
Color: White

Moon Sign: Libra
Moon enters Scorpio 12:55 pm
Incense: Cinnamon

26 Wednesday
St. Anne's Day
Waxing Moon
Moon phase: Second Quarter
Color: Yellow

Moon Sign: Scorpio
Incense: Lilac

27 Thursday
Sleepyhead Day (Finnish)
Waxing Moon
Moon phase: Second Quarter
Color: Crimson

Moon Sign: Scorpio
Moon enters Sagittarius 8:24 pm
Incense: Jasmine

28 Friday
Independence Day (Peruvian)
Waxing Moon
Moon phase: Second Quarter
Color: Rose

Moon Sign: Sagittarius
Incense: Mint

July

29 Saturday
St. Olaf Festival (Faroese)
Waxing Moon
Moon phase: Second Quarter
Color: Brown

Moon Sign: Sagittarius
Moon enters Capricorn 11:44 pm
Incense: Rue

---

30 Sunday
Micman Festival of St. Ann
Waxing Moon
Moon phase: Second Quarter
Color: Yellow

Moon Sign: Capricorn
Incense: Heliotrope

---

31 Monday
Feast of St. Ignatius
Waxing Moon
Moon phase: Second Quarter
Color: Silver

Moon Sign: Capricorn
Moon enters Aquarius 11:58 pm
Incense: Rosemary

July Correspondences

Stones: Turquoise, ruby
Animals: Dog, loon, woodpecker, salmon
Flowers: Larkspur, water lily
Deities: Danu, Demeter, Luna, Mercury, Parvati
Zodiac: Cancer

August

☺ **Tuesday**
Lammas
Waxing Moon
Full Moon 2:32 pm
Color: Maroon

Moon Sign: Aquarius
Incense: Basil

---

2 **Wednesday**
Porcingula (Pecos)
Waning Moon
Moon phase: Third Quarter
Color: Brown

Moon Sign: Aquarius
Moon enters Pisces 11:05 pm
Incense: Bay laurel

---

3 **Thursday**
Flag Day (Venezuelan)
Waning Moon
Moon phase: Third Quarter
Color: Green

Moon Sign: Pisces
Incense: Balsam

---

4 **Friday**
Constitution Day (Cook Islands)
Waning Moon
Moon phase: Third Quarter
Color: Coral

Moon Sign: Pisces
Moon enters Aries 11:19 pm
Incense: Rose

---

5 **Saturday**
Carnival of Bogotá
Waning Moon
Moon phase: Third Quarter
Color: Indigo

Moon Sign: Aries
Incense: Sage

---

6 **Sunday**
Hiroshima Peace Memorial Ceremony
Waning Moon
Moon phase: Third Quarter
Color: Orange

Moon Sign: Aries
Incense: Eucalyptus

---

7 **Monday**
Republic Day (Ivorian)
Waning Moon
Moon phase: Third Quarter
Color: Ivory

Moon Sign: Aries
Moon enters Taurus 2:25 am
Incense: Narcissus

August

Tuesday
Farmers' Day (Tanzanian)
Waning Moon
Fourth Quarter 6:28 am
Color: Black

Moon Sign: Taurus
Incense: Bayberry

---

9 Wednesday
Nagasaki Peace Memorial Ceremony
Waning Moon
Moon phase: Fourth Quarter
Color: Topaz

Moon Sign: Taurus
Moon enters Gemini 9:05 am
Incense: Lavender

---

10 Thursday
Puck Fair (ends Aug. 12; Irish)
Waning Moon
Moon phase: Fourth Quarter
Color: White

Moon Sign: Gemini
Incense: Carnation

---

11 Friday
Mountain Day (Japanese)
Waning Moon
Moon phase: Fourth Quarter
Color: Pink

Moon Sign: Gemini
Moon enters Cancer 6:52 pm
Incense: Thyme

---

12 Saturday
World Elephant Day
Waning Moon
Moon phase: Fourth Quarter
Color: Blue

Moon Sign: Cancer
Incense: Pine

---

13 Sunday
Women's Day (Tunisian)
Waning Moon
Moon phase: Fourth Quarter
Color: Gold

Moon Sign: Cancer
Incense: Almond

---

14 Monday
Independence Day (Pakistani)
Waning Moon
Moon phase: Fourth Quarter
Color: White

Moon Sign: Cancer
Moon enters Leo 6:36 am
Incense: Lily

August

15 Tuesday
Bon Festival (Japanese)
Waning Moon
Moon phase: Fourth Quarter
Color: Red

Moon Sign: Leo
Incense: Ylang-ylang

☽ Wednesday
Xicolatada (French)
Waning Moon
New Moon 5:38 am
Color: Yellow

Moon Sign: Leo
Moon enters Virgo 7:14 pm
Incense: Marjoram

---

17 Thursday
Black Cat Appreciation Day
Waxing Moon
Moon phase: First Quarter
Color: Crimson

Moon Sign: Virgo
Incense: Jasmine

---

18 Friday
St. Helen's Day
Waxing Moon
Moon phase: First Quarter
Color: White

Moon Sign: Virgo
Incense: Violet

---

19 Saturday
Vinalia Rustica (Roman)
Waxing Moon
Moon phase: First Quarter
Color: Brown

Moon Sign: Virgo
Moon enters Libra 7:53 am
Incense: Rue

---

20 Sunday
St. Stephen's Day (Hungarian)
Waxing Moon
Moon phase: First Quarter
Color: Amber

Moon Sign: Libra
Incense: Frankincense

---

21 Monday
Consualia (Roman)
Waxing Moon
Moon phase: First Quarter
Color: Lavender

Moon Sign: Libra
Moon enters Scorpio 7:22 pm
Incense: Clary sage

August

22 Tuesday
Qixi Festival (Chinese)
Waxing Moon
Moon phase: First Quarter
Color: Scarlet

Moon Sign: Scorpio
Incense: Geranium

23 Wednesday
National Day (Romanian)
Waxing Moon
Moon phase: First Quarter
Color: White

Moon Sign: Scorpio
Sun enters Virgo 5:01 am
Incense: Lilac

Thursday
St. Bartholomew's Day
Waxing Moon
Second Quarter 5:57 am
Color: Turquoise

Moon Sign: Cancer
Moon enters Sagittarius 4:07 am
Incense: Myrrh

25 Friday
Liberation of Paris
Waxing Moon
Moon phase: Second Quarter
Color: Purple

Moon Sign: Sagittarius
Incense: Vanilla

26 Saturday
Heroes' Day (Namibian)
Waxing Moon
Moon phase: Second Quarter
Color: Blue

Moon Sign: Sagottarius
Moon enters Capricorn 9:05 am
Incense: Ivy

27 Sunday
Independence Day (Moldovan)
Waxing Moon
Moon phase: Second Quarter
Color: Yellow

Moon Sign: Capricorn
Incense: Juniper

28 Monday
St. Augustine's Day
Waxing Moon
Moon phase: Second Quarter
Color: Silver

Moon Sign: Capricorn
Moon enters Aquarius 10:32 am
Incense: Rosemary

August

29 Tuesday

St. John's Beheading
Waxing Moon
Moon phase: Second Quarter
Color: Gray

Moon Sign: Aquarius
Incense: Ginger

 Wednesday

Ghost Festival (Chinese)
Waxing Moon
Full Moon 9:36 pm
Color: Topaz

Moon Sign: Aquarius
Moon enters Pisces 9:56 am
Incense: Honeysuckle

---

31 Thursday

La Tomatina (Valencian)
Waning Moon
Moon phase: Third Quarter
Color: Green

Moon Sign: Pisces
Incense: Nutmeg

August Corresondences

Stones: Peridot, carnelian
Animals: Crow, owl, sturgeon
Flowers: Gladiolus, poppy
Deities: Amaterasu, Helios, Sekhmet, Ra
Zodiac: Leo

September

℔

1 **Friday**
Wattle Day (Australian)
Waning Moon
Moon phase: Third Quarter
Color: Pink

Moon Sign: Pisces
Moon enters Aries 9:25 am
Incense: Cypress

---

2 **Saturday**
St. Mammes's Day
Waning Moon
Moon phase: Third Quarter
Color: Indigo

Moon Sign: Aries
Incense: Magnolia

---

3 **Sunday**
National Feast of San Marino
Waning Moon
Moon phase: Third Quarter
Color: Amber

Moon Sign: Aries
Moon enters Taurus 11:00 am
Incense: Hyacinth

---

4 **Monday**
Labor Day • Labour Day (Canadian)
Waning Moon
Moon phase: Third Quarter
Color: Gray

Moon Sign: Taurus
Incense: Hyssop

---

5 **Tuesday**
International Day of Charity
Waning Moon
Moon phase: Third Quarter
Color: Black

Moon Sign: Taurus
Moon enters Gemini 4:07 pm
Incense: Cedar

☾ **Wednesday**
Hiroshima Peace Memorial Ceremony
Waning Moon
Fourth Quarter 6:21 pm
Color: White

Moon Sign: Gemini
Incense: Lilac

---

7 **Thursday**
Independence Day (Brazilian)
Waning Moon
Moon phase: Fourth Quarter
Color: Purple

Moon Sign: Gemini
Incense: Carnation

September

♍

8 Friday
International Literacy Day
Waning Moon
Moon phase: Fourth Quarter
Color: Coral

Moon Sign: Gemini
Moon enters Cancer 1:00 am
Incense: Alder

9 Saturday
Remembrance for Herman the Cheruscan (Asatru)
Waning Moon
Moon phase: Fourth Quarter
Color: Blue

Moon Sign: Cancer
Incense: Patchouli

10 Sunday
Grandparents' Day
Waning Moon
Moon phase: Fourth Quarter
Color: Gold

Moon Sign: Cancer
Moon enters Leo 12:36 pm
Incense: Frankincense

11 Monday
Meditrinalia (Roman)
Waning Moon
Moon phase: Fourth Quarter
Color: White

Moon Sign: Leo
Incense: Lily

12 Tuesday
Mindfulness Day
Waning Moon
Moon phase: Fourth Quarter
Color: Maroon

Moon Sign: Leo
Incense: Basil

13 Wednesday
The Gods' Banquet
Waning Moon
Moon phase: Fourth Quarter
Color: Yellow

Moon Sign: Leo
Moon enters Virgo 1:18 am
Incense: Marjoram

☽ Thursday
Holy Cross Day
Waning Moon
New Moon 9:40 pm
Color: Green

Moon Sign: Virgo
Incense: Balsam

September

15 Friday

Rosh Hashanah begins at sundown
Waxing Moon
Moon phase: First Quarter
Color: Rose

Moon Sign: Virgo
Moon enters Libra 1:44 pm
Incense: Yarrow

16 Saturday

Independence Day (Mexican)
Waxing Moon
Moon phase: First Quarter
Color: Black

Moon Sign: Libra
Incense: Sandalwod

17 Sunday

Teachers' Day (Honduran)
Waxing Moon
Moon phase: First Quarter
Color: Yellow

Moon Sign: Libra
Incense: Heliotrope

18 Monday

World Water Monitoring Day
Waxing Moon
Moon phase: First Quarter
Color: Silver

Moon Sign: Libra
Moon enters Scorpio 12:58 am
Incense: Clary sage

19 Tuesday

Feast of San Gennaro
Waxing Moon
Moon phase: First Quarter
Color: Red

Moon Sign: Scorpio
Incense: Ylang-ylang

20 Wednesday

St. Eustace's Day
Waxing Moon
Moon phase: First Quarter
Color: Topaz

Moon Sign: Scorpio
Moon enters Sagittarius 10:06 pm
Incense: Lavender

21 Thursday

UN International Day of Peace
Waxing Moon
Moon phase: First Quarter
Color: Turquoise

Moon Sign: Sagittarius
Incense: Mulberry

September

☽ Friday
Hobbit Day
Waxing Moon
Second Quarter 3:32 pm
Color: Purple

Moon Sign: Sagittarius
Moon enters Capricorn 4:20 pm
Incense: Rose

---

23 Saturday
Mabon • Fall Equinox
Waxing Moon
Moon phase: Second Quarter
Color: Brown

Moon Sign: Capricorn
Sun enters Libra 2:50 am
Incense: Sage

---

24 Sunday
Yom Kippur begins at sundown
Waxing Moon
Moon phase: Second Quarter
Color: Orange

Moon Sign: Capricorn
Moon enters Aquarius 7:29 pm
Incense: Eucalyptus

---

25 Monday
Doll Memorial Service (Japanese)
Waxing Moon
Moon phase: Second Quarter
Color: Ivory

Moon Sign: Aquarius
Incense: Neroli

---

26 Tuesday
Feast of Santa Justina (Mexican)
Waxing Moon
Moon phase: Second Quarter
Color: White

Moon Sign: Aquarius
Moon enters Pisces 8:18 pm
Incense: Ginger

---

27 Wednesday
Meskel (Ethiopian and Eritrean)
Waxing Moon
Moon phase: Second Quarter
Color: Brown

Moon Sign: Pisces
Incense: Bay laurel

---

28 Thursday
Confucius's birthday
Waxing Moon
Moon phase: Second Quarter
Color: Green

Moon Sign: Pisces
Moon enters Aries 8:17 pm
Incense: Clove

September

♎︎

 Friday
Sukkot begins at sundown
Waxing Moon
Full Moon 5:58 am
Color: Pink

Moon Sign: Aries
Incense: Violet

---

30 Saturday
St. Jerome's Day
Waning Moon
Moon phase: Third Quarter
Color: Gray

Moon Sign: Aries
Moon enters Taurus 9:18 pm
Incense: Pine

September Correspondences

Stones: Sapphire, sardonyx, zircon
Animals: Bear, stag, fox
Flowers: Aster, morning glory
Deities: Frigg, Hestia, Persephone, Odin
Zodiac: Virgo

October

1 Sunday
Armed Forces Day (South Korean)
Waning Moon
Moon phase: Third Quarter
Color: Amber

Moon Sign: Taurus
Incense: Juniper

2 Monday
Gandhi's birthday
Waning Moon
Moon phase: Third Quarter
Color: Lavender

Moon Sign: Taurus
Incense: Lily

3 Tuesday
German Unity Day
Waning Moon
Moon phase: Third Quarter
Color: Maroon

Moon Sign: Taurus
Moon enters Gemini 1:03 am
Incense: Cinnamon

4 Wednesday
St. Francis's Day
Waning Moon
Moon phase: Third Quarter
Color: Yellow

Moon Sign: Gemini
Incense: Marjoram

5 Thursday
Republic Day (Portuguese)
Waning Moon
Moon phase: Third Quarter
Color: Crimson

Moon Sign: Gemini
Moon enters Cancer 8:32 am
Incense: Nutmeg

◐ Friday
Sukkot ends
Waning Moon
Fourth Quarter 9:48 am
Color: Rose

Moon Sign: Cancer
Incense: Cypress

7 Saturday
Nagasaki Kunchi Festival (ends Oct. 9)
Waning Moon
Moon phase: Fourth Quarter
Color: Blue

Moon Sign: Cancer
Moon enters Leo 7:24 pm
Incense: Patchouli

October

8 Sunday
Arbor Day (Namibian)
Waning Moon
Moon phase: Fourth Quarter
Color: Orange

Moon Sign: Leo
Incense: Almond

9 Monday
Indigenous Peoples' Day
Waning Moon
Moon phase: Fourth Quarter
Color: Silver

Moon Sign: Leo
Incense: Narcissus

10 Tuesday
Finnish Literature Day
Waning Moon
Moon phase: Fourth Quarter
Color: Black

Moon Sign: Leo
Moon enters Virgo 8:02 am
Incense: Bayberry

11 Wednesday
Meditrinalia (Roman)
Waning Moon
Moon phase: Fourth Quarter
Color: Brown

Moon Sign: Virgo
Incense: Honeysuckle

12 Thursday
National Festival of Spain
Waning Moon
Moon phase: Fourth Quarter
Color: Turquoise

Moon Sign: Virgo
Moon enters Libra 8:22 pm
Incense: Apricot

13 Friday
Fontinalia (Roman)
Waning Moon
Moon phase: Fourth Quarter
Color: White

Moon Sign: Libra
Incense: Alder

Saturday
National Education Day (Polish)
Waning Moon
New Moon 1:55 pm
Color: Gray

Moon Sign: Libra
Incense: Rue

October

15 Sunday
The October Horse (Roman)
Waxing Moon
Moon phase: First Quarter
Color: Gold

Moon Sign: Libra
Moon enters Scorpio 7:04 am
Incense: Marigold

---

16 Monday
Dessalines Day (Haitian)
Waxing Moon
Moon phase: First Quarter
Color: Ivory

Moon Sign: Scorpio
Incense: Rosemary

---

17 Tuesday
Dessalines Day (Haitian)
Waxing Moon
Moon phase: First Quarter
Color: Scarlet

Moon Sign: Scorpio
Moon enters Sagittarius 3:36 pm
Incense: Geranium

---

18 Wednesday
Feast of St. Luke
Waxing Moon
Moon phase: First Quarter
Color: Topaz

Moon Sign: Sagittarius
Incense: Lilac

---

19 Thursday
Mother Teresa Day (Albanian)
Waxing Moon
Moon phase: First Quarter
Color: Purple

Moon Sign: Sagittarius
Moon enters Capricorn 9:55 pm
Incense: Balsam

---

20 Friday
Feast of St. Acca
Waxing Moon
Moon phase: First Quarter
Color: Coral

Moon Sign: Capricorn
Incense: Mint

◖ Saturday
Apple Day (United Kingdom)
Waxing Moon
Second Quarter 11:29 pm
Color: Indigo

Moon Sign: Capricorn
Incense: Sandalwood

22 Sunday
Jidai Festival (Japanese)
Waxing Moon
Moon phase: Second Quarter
Color: Amber

Moon Sign: Capricorn
Moon enters Aquarius 2:06 am
Incense: Hyacinth

23 Monday
Double Ninth Festival (Chinese)
Waxing Moon
Moon phase: Second Quarter
Color: Gray

Moon Sign: Aquarius
Sun enters Scorpio 12:21 pm
Incense: Hyssop

24 Tuesday
St. Crispin's Day
Waxing Moon
Moon phase: Second Quarter
Color: Red

Moon Sign: Aquarius
Moon enters Pisces 4:33 am
Incense: Cedar

25 Wednesday
St. Crispin's Day
Waxing Moon
Moon phase: Second Quarter
Color: White

Moon Sign: Pisces
Incense: Lavender

26 Thursday
Death of Alfred the Great
Waxing Moon
Moon phase: Second Quarter
Color: Green

Moon Sign: Pisces
Moon enters Aries 6:02 am
Incense: Jasmine

27 Friday
Feast of St. Abbán
Waxing Moon
Moon phase: Second Quarter
Color: Pink

Moon Sign: Aries
Incense: Thyme

Saturday
Ohi Day (Greek)
Waxing Moon
Full Moon 4:24 pm
Color: Blue

Moon Sign: Aries
Moon enters Taurus 7:44 am
Incense: Ivy

October

29 Sunday

National Cat Day
Waning Moon
Moon phase: Third Quarter
Color: Yellow

Moon Sign: Taurus
Incense: Heliotrope

---

30 Monday

John Adams's birthday
Waning Moon
Moon phase: Third Quarter
Color: White

Moon Sign: Taurus
Moon enters Gemini 11:08 pm
Incense: Neroli

---

31 Tuesday

Halloween • Samhain
Waning Moon
Moon phase: Third Quarter
Color: Maroon

Moon Sign: Gemini
Incense: Ylang-ylang

October Correpondences

Stones: Opal, tourmaline
Animals: Bat, rat, crow, raven, dove
Flower: Calendula
Deities: Athena, Cernunnos, Hephaestus,
Shiva, Venus
Zodiac: Libra

November

1 Wednesday
All Saints' Day • Día de los Muertos
Waning Moon
Moon phase: Third Quarter
Color: Topaz

Moon Sign: Gemini
Moon enters Cancer 5:30 pm
Incense: Bay laurel

2 Thursday
All Souls' Day
Waning Moon
Moon phase: Third Quarter
Color: Turquoise

Moon Sign: Cancer
Incense: Myrrh

3 Friday
Culture Day (Japanese)
Waning Moon
Moon phase: Third Quarter
Color: Purple

Moon Sign: Cancer
Incense: Violet

4 Saturday
Mischief Night (British)
Waning Moon
Moon phase: Third Quarter
Color: Gray

Moon Sign: Cancer
Moon enters Leo 3:21 am
Incense: Sage

◖ Sunday
Guy Fawkes Night (British)
Waning Moon
Fourth Quarter 3:37 am
Color: Gold

Moon Sign: Leo
Incense: Almond

Daylight Saving Time ends at 2 am

6 Monday
St. Leonard's Ride (German)
Waning Moon
Moon phase: Fourth Quarter
Color: Silver

Moon Sign: Leo
Moon enters Virgo 2:39 pm
Incense: Clary sage

7 Tuesday
Election Day (general)
Waning Moon
Moon phase: Fourth Quarter
Color: Black

Moon Sign: Virgo
Incense: Cinnamon

November ♏

8 Wednesday

World Urbanism Day
Waning Moon
Moon phase: Fourth Quarter
Color: White

Moon Sign: Virgo
Incense: Honeysuckle

9 Thursday

Fateful Day (German)
Waning Moon
Moon phase: Fourth Quarter
Color: Purple

Moon Sign: Virgo
Moon enters Libra 3:08 am
Incense: Mulberry

10 Friday

Martin Luther's Birthday
Waning Moon
Moon phase: Fourth Quarter
Color: Rose

Moon Sign: Libra
Incense: Vanilla

11 Saturday

Veterans Day • Remembrance Day (Canadian)
Waning Moon
Moon phase: Fourth Quarter
Color: Blue

Moon Sign: Libra
Moon enters Scorpio 1:39 pm
Incense: Magnolia

12 Sunday

Diwali
Waning Moon
Moon phase: Fourth Quarter
Color: Yellow

Moon Sign: Scorpio
Incense: Frankincense

☽ Monday

Festival of Jupiter
Waning Moon
New Moon 4:27 am
Color: Ivory

Moon Sign: Scorpio
Moon enters Sagittarius 9:23 pm
Incense: Hyssop

14 Tuesday

Feast of St. Lawrence O'Toole
Waxing Moon
Moon phase: First Quarter
Color: Maroon

Moon Sign: Sagittarius
Incense: Geranium

15 Wednesday
King's Feast (Belgian)
Waxing Moon
Moon phase: First Quarter
Color: Brown

Moon Sign: Sagittarius
Incense: Lilac

---

16 Thursday
St. Margaret of Scotland's Day
Waxing Moon
Moon phase: First Quarter
Color: Green

Moon Sign: Sagittarius
Moon enters Capricorn 2:41 am
Incense: Jasmine

---

17 Friday
Native American Heritage Day
Waxing Moon
Moon phase: First Quarter
Color: Coral

Moon Sign: Capricorn
Incense: Alder

---

18 Saturday
National Adoption Day
Waxing Moon
Moon phase: First Quarter
Color: Black

Moon Sign: Capricorn
Moon enters Aquarius 6:28 am
Incense: Pine

---

19 Sunday
Garifuna Settlement Day (Belizean)
Waxing Moon
Moon phase: First Quarter
Color: Amber

Moon Sign: Aquarius
Incense: Juniper

◐ Monday
Revolution Day (Mexican)
Waxing Moon
Second Quarter 5:50 am
Color: Lavender

Moon Sign: Aquarius
Moon enters Pisces 9:29 am
Incense: Lily

---

21 Tuesday
Feast of the Presentation of Mary
Waxing Moon
Moon phase: Second Quarter
Color: Gray

Moon Sign: Pisces
Incense: Basil

November

22 Wednesday
St. Cecilia's Day
Waxing Moon
Moon phase: Second Quarter
Color: Yellow

Moon Sign: Pisces
Sun enters Sagittarius 9:03 am
Moon enters Aries 12:19 pm
Incense: Marjoram

23 Thursday
Thanksgiving Day (US)
Waxing Moon
Moon phase: Second Quarter
Color: Crimson

Moon Sign: Aries
Incense: Clove

24 Friday
Evolution Day
Waxing Moon
Moon phase: Second Quarter
Color: Pink

Moon Sign: Aries
Moon enters Taurus 3:29 pm
Incense: Orchid

25 Saturday
Feast of St. Catherine of Alexandria
Waxing Moon
Moon phase: Second Quarter
Color: Indigo

Moon Sign: Taurus
Incense: Ivy

26 Sunday
Constitution Day (Indian)
Waxing Moon
Moon phase: Second Quarter
Color: Orange

Moon Sign: Taurus
Moon enters Gemini 7:40 pm
Incense: Hyacinth

Monday
Feast of St. Virgilius
Waxing Moon
Full Moon 4:16 am
Color: Gray

Moon Sign: Gemini
Incense: Rosemary

28 Tuesday
Republic Day (Chadian)
Waning Moon
Moon phase: Third Quarter
Color: Red

Moon Sign: Gemini
Incense: Ginger

November

29 Wednesday
William Tubman's birthday (Liberian)
Waning Moon
Moon phase: Third Quarter
Color: Topaz

Moon Sign: Gemini
Moon enters Cancer 1:54 am
Incense: Lavender

30 Thursday
St. Andrew's Day (Scottish)
Waning Moon
Moon phase: Third Quarter
Color: White

Moon Sign: Cancer
Incense: Nutmeg

November Correspondences

Stones: Citrine, cat's eye, topaz
Animals: Snake, eel, goose, raccoon
Flower: Chrysanthemum
Deities: Anubis, Inanna, Kali, Pluto
Zodiac: Scorpio

December

1 Friday
Feast for Death of Aleister Crowley (Thelemic)
Waning Moon
Moon phase: Third Quarter
Color: Coral

Moon Sign: Cancer
Moon enters Leo 11:00 am
Incense: Mint

---

2 Saturday
Republic Day (Laotian)
Waning Moon
Moon phase: Third Quarter
Color: Blue

Moon Sign: Leo
Incense: Sandalwood

---

3 Sunday
St. Francis Xavier's Day
Waning Moon
Moon phase: Third Quarter
Color: Yellow

Moon Sign: Leo
Moon enters Virgo 10:50 pm
Incense: Eucalyptus

---

4 Monday
Feasts of Shango and St. Barbara
Waning Moon
Moon phase: Third Quarter
Color: Ivory

Moon Sign: Virgo
Incense: Neroli

☽ Tuesday
Krampus Night (European)
Waning Moon
Fourth Quarter 12:49 am
Color: Scarlet

Moon Sign: Virgo
Incense: Bayberry

---

6 Wednesday
St. Nicholas's Day
Waning Moon
Moon phase: Fourth Quarter
Color: Brown

Moon Sign: Virgo
Moon enters Libra 11:35 am
Incense: Lilac

---

7 Thursday
Hanukkah begins at sundown
Waning Moon
Moon phase: Fourth Quarter
Color: Green

Moon Sign: Libra
Incense: Carnation

December

8 **Friday**
Bodhi Day (Japanese)
Waning Moon
Moon phase: Fourth Quarter
Color: Pink

Moon Sign: Libra
Moon enters Scorpio 10:35 pm
Incense: Rose

9 **Saturday**
Anna's Day (Swedish)
Waning Moon
Moon phase: Fourth Quarter
Color: Black

Moon Sign: Scorpio
Incense: Rue

10 **Sunday**
Alfred Nobel Day
Waning Moon
Moon phase: Fourth Quarter
Color: Orange

Moon Sign: Scorpio
Incense: Marigold

11 **Monday**
Pilgrimage at Tortugas
Waning Moon
Moon phase: Fourth Quarter
Color: Silver

Moon Sign: Scorpio
Moon enters Sagittarius 6:11 am
Incense: Narcissus

☽ **Tuesday**
Fiesta of Our Lady of Guadalupe (Mexican)
Waning Moon
New Moon 6:32 pm
Color: Red

Moon Sign: Sagittarius
Incense: Basil

13 **Wednesday**
St. Lucy's Day (Scandinavian and Italian)
Waxing Moon
Moon phase: First Quarter
Color: White

Moon Sign: Sagittarius
Moon enters Capricorn 10:31 am
Incense: Bay laurel

14 **Thursday**
Forty-Seven Ronin Memorial (Japanese)
Waxing Moon
Moon phase: First Quarter
Color: Purple

Moon Sign: Capricorn
Incense: Apricot

December

15 Friday
Hanukkah ends
Waxing Moon
Moon phase: First Quarter
Color: Rose

Moon Sign: Capricorn
Moon enters Aquarius 12:56 pm
Incense: Cypress

---

16 Saturday
Las Posadas begin (end Dec. 24)
Waxing Moon
Moon phase: First Quarter
Color: Indigo

Moon Sign: Aquarius
Incense: Ivy

---

17 Sunday
Saturnalia (Roman)
Waxing Moon
Moon phase: First Quarter
Color: Gold

Moon Sign: Aquarius
Moon enters Pisces 2:58 pm
Incense: Heliotrope

---

18 Monday
Feast of the Virgin of Solitude
Waxing Moon
Moon phase: First Quarter
Color: White

Moon Sign: Pisces
Incense: Lily

◑ Tuesday
Opalia (Roman)
Waxing Moon
Second Quarter 1:39 pm
Color: Maroon

Moon Sign: Pisces
Moon enters Aries 5:47 pm
Incense: Cinnamon

---

20 Wednesday
Feast of St. Dominic of Silos
Waxing Moon
Moon phase: Second Quarter
Color: Yellow

Moon Sign: Aries
Incense: Honeysuckle

---

21 Thursday
Yule • Winter Solstice
Waxing Moon
Moon phase: Second Quarter
Color: Turquoise

Moon Sign: Aries
Sun enters Capricorn 10:27 pm
Moon enters Taurus 9:50 pm
Incense: Balsam

22 Friday

Feasts of SS. Chaeremon and Ischyrion
Waxing Moon
Moon phase: Second Quarter
Color: Coral

Moon Sign: Taurus
Incense: Alder

23 Friday

Larentalia (Roman)
Waxing Moon
Moon phase: Second Quarter
Color: Gray

Moon Sign: Taurus
Incense: Pine

24 Sunday

Christmas Eve
Waxing Moon
Moon phase: Second Quarter
Color: Amber

Moon Sign: Taurus
Moon enters Gemini 3:15 am
Incense: Frankincense

25 Monday

Christmas Day
Waxing Moon
Moon phase: Second Quarter
Color: Ivory

Moon Sign: Gemini
Incense: Rosemary

☺ Tuesday

Kwanzaa begins • Boxing Day
Waxing Moon
Full Moon 7:33 pm
Color: Gray

Moon Sign: Gemini
Moon enters Cancer 10:15 am
Incense: Cedar

27 Wednesday

St. Stephen's Day
Waning Moon
Moon phase: Third Quarter
Color: Topaz

Moon Sign: Cancer
Incense: Lavender

28 Thursday

Feast of the Holy Innocents
Waning Moon
Moon phase: Third Quarter
Color: Crimson

Moon Sign: Cancer
Moon enters Leo 7:23 pm
Incense: Mulberry

December

29 Friday
Feast of St. Thomas à Becket
Waning Moon
Moon phase: Third Quarter
Color: White

Moon Sign: Leo
Incense: Orchid

30 Saturday
Republic Day (Madagascan)
Waning Moon
Moon phase: Third Quarter
Color: Blue

Moon Sign: Leo
Incense: Magnolia

31 Sunday
New Year's Eve
Waning Moon
Moon phase: Third Quarter
Color: Orange

Moon Sign: Aries
Moon enters Virgo 6:53 am
Incense: Juniper

December Correpondences

Stones: Turquoise, onyx, bloodstone, blue topaz
Animals: Elk, horse, stag, reindeer
Flowers: Narcissus
Deities: Artemis, Jupiter, Rhiannon, Thor
Zodiac: Sagittarius

Fire Magic

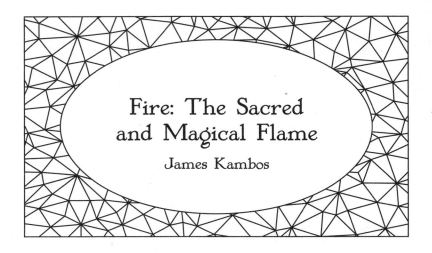

Fire: The Sacred and Magical Flame

James Kambos

Awe and wonder. Fear and respect. These are only a few of the emotions the element fire and its sacred flame have stirred in the human heart and mind since prehistoric times. Fire has played a key role in the development of civilization and magic since the first hearth was just a cave floor.

All of us can remember a time from our past when fire helped create a special memory for us. Maybe it was the candles on a birthday cake, candles being lit during a holiday, or perhaps a campfire. I too have special memories of fire and the feeling it created in me as a child. My earliest memories of fire are the feelings of comfort and warmth it created.

The winters I spent on my grandparents' Ohio farm helped create some of those memories. The winters in the northern Ohio farmlands could be brutal and come early. The wind would howl and usually carried with it snow. It would leave deep drifts, making trips to the woodpile difficult. But my grandparents managed to build a fire in the living room's brick fireplace. They would keep it burning for days. It was a treat to curl up in front of the fire with my faithful spaniel Brownie. When I was a teen, my parents built their dream home. The great room featured a massive brick fireplace with a rustic sycamore beam as its mantle. It was about this time that my parents divorced. Looking for comfort, I found myself drawn to the fireplace on fall and winter evenings. I'd lay a fire and watch the flames. The fire gave me comfort and even a feeling of companionship during that troubled time.

Today, my own home, I'm happy to say, has a woodstove. Beginning in late fall, I use my stove as a heat source during the coldest months. Not only does it heat my home, but it still gives me that sense of comfort I knew long ago. On winter nights when I'm alone writing late into the night, my fire keeps me company, as well as being my magical companion.

I understand now why so many magicians believe that of all the elements, fire is the one that is most nearly alive. When the wood in my stove burns, hisses, and crackles, it does seem to be speaking to me.

So, whether you simply burn a candle or build a bonfire, as long as you have some form of fire, you're never really alone!

Fire: A Brief History

The history of fire—when it began on Earth, when it was first seen, and when our ancestors first learned how to create and control fire—are questions that still don't have definite answers. Historians and archaeologists are still making educated guesses about fire's exact origins. We are relatively sure that Earth's atmosphere couldn't support or produce fire until about 400 million years ago. The reason for this is Earth's atmosphere at first didn't contain enough oxygen to sustain fire. Gradually, however, active volcanoes releasing certain gasses and an increase in the growth of vegetation helped create an atmosphere on Earth favorable for the creation of fire.

Earth's first fires were likely nature related in origin. Fires were probably first caused by lightning strikes igniting any dry forest debris, wood, bark, leaves, and the like.

At some point 1 million to 1.6 million years ago, our early ancestors learned how to create and maintain simple campfires. Flint, rocks, twigs, and bark were most likely used to build and sustain these fires. But we know one thing for certain. At the moment our distant upright, two-legged kin first struck that flint and rock together, igniting a mere pile of twigs and leaves, the course of all humanity was changed forever. It was then, when that first man-made spark burst into the first sacred flame, that every human—then, now, and until the end of time—would be lifted above all other forms of animal life. Thanks to some brave person with the will to experiment, the human race became the supreme being of planet Earth.

The impact of that moment changed human history and its future forever. Humans became mobile and were able to live in different regions and climates. The flame enabled humans to defend themselves against the fang of the wild beast and the bite of cold and ice. Health improved. Meats and vegetables were able to be cooked, which killed harmful bacteria.

And during the long, dark nights, early humans gathered around the first primitive hearth, the cave floor. In the shadows of those flickering flames, friendships were kindled. An emotion known as love began. From that love, relationships and clans were formed. The clans became villages, then cities. From the cities, nations were created. Eventually, nations combined to form empires. And the empires finally spread their civilizations through every continent.

Think about it. It all began with an ember, a spark, and a magical flame.

The Gift of Fire

The human race has been fascinated with fire since early humans saw flashes of lightning for the first time. Those flashes of "fire in the sky" inspired awe, fear, and wonder in our ancient ancestors. Then, when humans realized that they could create and control fire, those feelings of wonder gave way to a sense of power and mastery. As soon as the human race realized the importance of this sacred flame, we became natural fire tenders.

Soon the ancients began to ask themselves, how did they become blessed with this sacred element? Where did it come from?

The search for answers began. Fire had become such a vital part of human existence that many ancient civilizations began to view fire as a divine gift. Soon, fire creation stories began to be told in various civilizations. These stories became myths and legends. The myths are as diverse as the societies that created them. But these fire creation myths have something in common: they helped lay the groundwork for what would eventually become more organized forms of faith, religion, and magic.

Here is one example of a fire creation myth from ancient Greece. This myth centers around the giant Greek Titan god Prometheus.

In this version, Prometheus had an argument with Zeus, the ruler of the gods and humanity. Prometheus claimed that Zeus had been unfair to humans and that he refused to share many of the comforts the gods possessed. Zeus refused to listen to this argument. But Prometheus was determined to share a divine gift with the human race. The gift he chose was fire. Prometheus became a hero to humankind. Zeus, however, was outraged, and he chained Prometheus to a mountain peak. Every day for centuries, an eagle (a symbol of Zeus) would attack Prometheus and devour his liver. His liver would regenerate itself, but the attacks continued. Finally, the hero-god Heracles, the son of Zeus, thought Prometheus had suffered enough. Heracles destroyed the eagle and freed Prometheus.

This fire creation myth shows us two things. First, it tells us that fire is viewed as an element that gives comfort to human existence. And second, it shows us that the ancients held fire in such high regard that they believed fire must have evolved from a divine source.

Even today, fire still captures our imagination.

The Magic of Fire

Fire magic and fire itself still captivate us after all these ages. Why? Perhaps it's an instinct or maybe it's some misty race memory. Or it could be a secret held in the glowing embers of every fire that has ever burned. For some reason, our kinship with fire continues into modern times.

The simple act of lighting a candle still evokes feelings of magic, mystery, romance, and spiritual peace in most of us. Lighting a candle in church and offering a prayer and lighting a candle during the Jewish observance of Hanukkah show how widely fire is used among different faiths.

To Pagans, fire also has special significance. The element fire is found on the ritual altar in various forms during magical and spiritual rites. A burning candle is one way a magician or Witch includes fire during rituals. The glow of incense and a small fire in a cauldron are other ways fire may be utilized by Pagans. Also, the four cardinal points are frequently marked by burning candles in the magic circle.

But the most important reason fire is used by modern Witches and Pagans is because fire creates an atmosphere that allows magic to happen. When you perform a ritual or cast a spell by candlelight or firelight, you create an aura where magic can take place. The simple act of lighting one candle can transform an ordinary room into an enchanting space—a space where the extraordinary can happen. In a candlelit room even the features of the magician can take on a mystical appearance.

When you perform any type of fire magic, you're working with a form of magic that has been in existence since before recorded history.

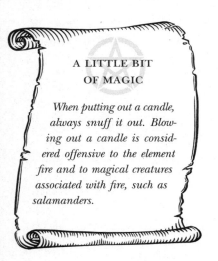

A LITTLE BIT OF MAGIC

When putting out a candle, always snuff it out. Blowing out a candle is considered offensive to the element fire and to magical creatures associated with fire, such as salamanders.

Fire Spells

Here are three fire/candle spells. They focus on three popular topics—love, breaking a curse, and fire gazing, which is a form of divination. These are only a few examples of fire magic. You may also use fire magic to contact a spirit, during meditation, or to cleanse a space.

This sentient element has much to share with us.

A Fire Love Spell

You'll need a red taper candle, a few drops of rose water, and a red cloth. Rub the rose water along the candle as you think of your intent. Now follow the instructions in this verse:

Over your altar spread
A cloth of brightest red.
Light a red candle to illuminate the dark.
Let it burn, let it spark.

Next, say,

Fire, fire, child of the Sun,
Bring to me the perfect one.
Bring me away from darkness and into the light.
Let this candle burn against the night.

Allow the candle to burn out safely. When cool, wrap what's left of the candle in the cloth. Hide this bundle. When love comes to you, respectfully dispose of the candle and cloth.

Break a Curse Spell

Curses can be broken and reversed. For this spell you'll need some small twigs; however, you must save one twig and not burn it right away. Begin by starting a small fire with your twigs in a heatproof dish, cauldron, fireplace, or woodstove. Holding the twig you've saved, project your emotions into it as you say,

I now return this curse.
This evil I now reverse.

All evil be turned,
All evil be burned!

Break the twig you're holding into small pieces, and cast them
into the fire. In a strong voice announce,

Guardians of the east, west, north, and south, help me destroy this
curse in the fire's mouth.

Watch as the twig is consumed by the fire, turning the curse into
useless ashes.

Leave the ashes alone for three days. On the fourth day, scatter
the ashes upon the ground. Now Mother Earth will absorb any lingering evil and neutralize the curse's power.

A Fire Gazing Ritual

Fire gazing, or scrying by fire, is the oldest form of fire magic. Its of-
ficial name is pyromancy, and it's been used for thousands of years.

You may perform it by gazing into the flame of one candle or into a blazing fireplace fire. It's up to you. For this ritual, I am using a candle, since many people don't have a fireplace. I think it's most effective when done at night. You'll need a new white taper candle. To draw psychic energy, it helps to also have a few dried leaves of sage on hand.

Begin by carefully lighting the candle. Sprinkle the dried sage around the base of the candle. Darken the room. Sit before the candle. Think of a question, and say these words:

Burning candle tall and white,
Answer my question on this night.
Let the answer come in any disguise;
May it appear before my eyes.
Let me see my answer in the flame,
Be it an image, a face, or a name.

Gaze intently at the flame, thinking of your question. The answer may come in many ways. You might see an entire scene or clues such as a number, letter, or a face. Keep your sessions short at first, perhaps 10 minutes. Snuff out the candle when done and discard the sage. You may use the candle again since it's now attuned to your energy.

· · · ☾ · · ·

From flint and bark to digital thermostat. From the first lightning flash to a candle flame on a Witch's altar. From a faint flicker of light on a cave floor to the nighttime glitter of a big city skyline, fire has paralleled the development of human history.

On long cold nights as I build my fire in my woodstove, I can see into our distant past. In the dancing flames, like the ones I tend now, friendships began, and the seeds of what would become known as society were nurtured. And at evening's end in the glowing embers I bank for the night are the memories of warmth, comfort, and magic that have accompanied the human race on its incredible journey from cave to city. Amazing—it all began with a spark, a flame.

Nightmare Protection

Diana Rajchel

Several years ago, a non-practitioner friend reached out to me. He and his wife had recently adopted a child born in Kosovo, and the boy had asked for a dream catcher after seeing a character on his dad's favorite show talk about one on television. No one from the family was Native. As the Witch they happened to know, I was asked because I tended to know about mystical solutions to some of life's problems. I asked the father a few questions about why his son wanted one—Did he think they were cool? What about the show and what it said about dream catchers got his attention? At first, the little boy just said he wanted one, but after a little prodding, the truth came out. He was still having nightmares from his time and losses in Kosovo. Given the inexpressible horrors that marked his early life, if anyone would need a dream catcher, it was this kid.

I am not one to leave a child to suffer, even if stopping that suffering might feel loaded to the adults. Using the information I had at the time, I connected his father to Native crafters who lived nearby, walked him through how to care for the dream catchers properly (there is a tradition that involves regular cleaning), and hoped that his son got all the help needed for his bad dreams.

Several years later, I found myself raising two boys in the middle of a pandemic. Both talked at length about anxieties from 2020 and struggled with upheaval in their lives that happened before the lockdown. Nightmares and avoiding sleep became regular features of their lives. While sometimes the cause was tween and adolescent mischief, other times it was feelings, fears, and the stress that comes with being a kid who has no say in any of the stuff happening. We did all the things parents on a tight budget with shared custody can do, but we needed a little magical help. Dream catchers were not an option. Even though the boys have

Native ancestry, their roots traced to different practices. So, as the household Witch, I needed to develop our own way to address the problem. After all, there are only so many times you can tell a scared kid, "Go to bed. I'm tired!"

The Causes of Nightmares

As it turns out, there are several magical ways to address nightmares—but for permanent resolution, you need to understand the root to resolve it. From a spiritual perspective, the causes of nightmares fall into three categories: physical causes (bad food, usually), emotional causes (after witnessing trauma or experiencing stress), and spiritual causes (spirit visitations, spells, etc.). As it turns out, the array of nightmare-dispelling magic addresses each of these categories. Once you know what sort of nightmare you are dealing with, you can use a magical charm as a remedy.

Physical Causes

Physical causes of nightmares call for pragmatic solutions. For example, eating a sugary snack less than two hours before bed can cause an upset stomach, so keep the night snacks refined sugar free. Too much noise and distraction can feed the brain the wrong material for the nighttime brain viewing. Sometimes, in places with thin walls, hearing neighbors (or feeling their energy) can cause bad reactions in sensitive people. Improving the sleep environment can mitigate bad sleep and nightmares. If possible, invest in blackout curtains and add a white noise machine to the bedroom. Choose sheets made from a material that feels pleasant against the skin. Reducing stressful stimuli during sleep does cut down on sleep itself becoming stressful.

A gentle exercise regimen an hour before bed also helps sleep quality. Simple yoga poses, such as cat-cow and child's pose, allow the release and grounding of excess energy. Also, a nice cup of tea may be a hard sell to the kiddos, but flavored just right (say, with a tiny bit of milk and cocoa powder), it can become a pleasant before-bed ritual.

An example of such a tea might use this formula, composed of herbs known for their soothing impact:

NIGHTMARE STOPPER TEA RECIPE
4 teaspoons lavender bud
2 teaspoons passionflower
2 teaspoons damiana
1 teaspoon catnip

Steep for 5 minutes in hot but not boiling water. For best effect, stir in a little bit of oat milk (oats have a relaxing quality) and sweeten with monk fruit or stevia glycerin. All the herbs promote relaxation—and they taste good compared to common sleep-inducing herbs like valerian and mugwort.

Emotional Causes
Emotionally caused nightmares are often the trickiest to address. Sometimes kids can't express what troubles them, and while a nice tea can calm the stress, it may not help with serious issues. Encouraging kids to find healthy ways to express their feelings can go a long way in cutting down night terrors, but sometimes they need a little bit more help.

When my teenager had a recurring nightmare for a week, I taught him a method I use for my recurring nightmares: bring it up while you're awake. He kept dreaming about a masked, menacing figure chasing him through the woods. When he told me about the problem, we discussed a method for confronting them. I told him to conjure the dream while awake, and then, while awake and in control of the dream, to snatch the mask off the face of the mysterious figure. It took him a few tries, but he eventually caught the miscreant. In dreamland, his little brother was playing a prank. He had the dream one more time that night. In his dream, he told his brother to knock it off, the dream shifted, and those nightmares stopped.

Sometimes, however, our kids have more nebulous emotional causes that don't result in recurring dreams. In those situations, they need just a little extra magic. My kids don't fare well with dream pillows—they find them "weird." However, they love their stuffed animals, and as it turns out, teddy bears have a North American history as expressions of President Teddy Roosevelt's compassion. When I found one of the kids' teddy bears with a hole in it, I thought of this bit of folklore and had an idea: Why not make it a nightmare protector? I went to my local crystal shop and picked up some citrine because it recharges continuously, smoky quartz for protection, and amethyst to heal any lingering emotional pains. I added a small bit of mugwort (to aid sleep), bay leaf (to invite dreams), and hops (to soothe nerves) and stitched up the little bear. Then I sat with the bear for a few days and talked to it as though it connected to the spirit of Brown Bear, and I explained how I wanted it to help my child.

Now my kiddo has a teddy bear he thought lost back with him in his bed, growling the nightmares away. The citrine inside continuously recharges the other crystals, so I won't need to perform update surgeries or anoint Buddy Bear with anything that might smell strange enough to get him removed from the bedroom.

Spiritual Causes for Nightmares

Spiritual causes for nightmares happen more for adults than for children. I once worked in a women's shelter where one woman's ex used sorcery specific to his culture in order to torment the children as a means of punishing her. I could always tell when the kids got their bad-dream visits by the feeling of fear and ick that rushed over me when I passed by their room at night. I was newer to magic at that time, so I used what I knew to help. I resorted to chi balls (balls of energy generated from my body and the environment around me) and filled them with a nightmare-stopping

intention. The people tormenting those kids hadn't planned for someone trying to stop them. The mother reported no nightmares that night, and not long after, they stopped altogether. I don't know whether I helped, whether the kids adjusted, or whether the mother found someone in her culture to help her. I hope all the above contributed.

For myself, I use a glass of water with a piece of camphor in it to reduce spirit visitations and messages, a method I learned from reading Draja Mickaharic's book *Spiritual Cleansing*. The water traps metaphysical drek while I sleep. In the morning, I flush the water down the toilet, rinse the glass, and refill it. If nightmares persist despite the water, I appeal to someone perceived as a scary part of the night. Praying to Hecate, for example, adds a touch of spiritual intervention when nocturnal visitations try to carry me away.

Conclusion

Every culture has people in it who suffer from nightmares. While dream catchers garner the most attention for solving this problem, the global collection of folklore offers a world of additional options to try and spirits to work with to stem frightening visions in the night. We have an added advantage in our day and age because we understand just a little bit more about the human brain and about the roots of nightmares, and that allows us to adjust our magic to the cause, rather than to just the general condition. Sleep well this night, and every night!

Resources

"History of Teddy Bears." Carnegie Museum of Natural History. Accessed January 3, 2022. https://carnegiemnh.org/history -of-teddy-bears/.

Mickaharic, Draja. *Spiritual Cleansing: A Handbook of Psychic Self-Protection.* Newburyport, MA: Weiser, 1982.

Connecting to the Divine Self

Stephanie Woodfield

The vast majority of my personal practices revolve around building a connection to the Divine. That connection to the sacred helps me navigate difficult times, heal old wounds, and find a sense of purpose and joy in life. Sometimes that connection is built in ritual, spending time in nature, meditating, or through prayer. Prayer is one of my go-to practices, mostly because it is fairly versatile. It can have structure or can be something freeform, such as sitting in front of my altar or in my car after a particularly hard day and just speaking candidly to the Divine. Prayer reminds me that the sacred isn't just around when I'm engaging in ritual, that it is present all around me all the time, and most importantly, that I can interact with the sacred at any time.

As I delved into creating my own prayer practice for the deities I honor, I realized I had been missing something essential. Myself. The more I focused on connecting to the sacred outside of myself, the message I kept receiving was the same: "See me within yourself." As the old maxim goes: as within, so without. To truly honor the Divine, I needed to see the Divine within myself. It's easy to be in awe of a deity—these are the forces that created the universe and keep all life in motion, hold vast wisdom, and can move and shape our lives in amazing ways. What isn't as easy to recognize is that piece of the sacred that lives within ourselves. We know all our own flaws and faults, and the world is quick to remind us of all our shortcomings. So often we are told we are not good enough, and many times we devalue ourselves as a result. Seeing our own value can be, not surprisingly, very hard. Part of why I felt I needed to connect more deeply with the Divine was to conquer those inner voices that whispered that I wasn't good enough and never would be. It felt somewhat ironic that the message from the Divine I was receiving was to look within, the very place I was trying to avoid looking. We forget that we are sacred. I began thinking of ways I could acknowledge the sacred within myself using the same methods I had been using to connect to the gods.

We find the concept of a portion of the Divine being bestowed on creation in mythology and spirituality around the world. In creation myths, the gods or divine source creates life by passing on a piece of their essence. Very often this essence is described as the "breath" of the divinity. If you practice Kabbalah, you might be familiar with the *rauch* (roo-akh), which in Hebrew means "breath," "wind," or "spirit." The rauch, or breath of the Divine, is what animated life. Askr and Embla, the first man and woman in Norse mythology, share a similar creation myth. The pair were created from driftwood found by the gods Odin, Vili, and Ve on the seashore. Odin gave them breath, Vili gave them reasoning, and Ve shaped them, giving them form. Whether we call this gifted piece of the Divine a spark or a breath, it all boils down to the concept that some piece of you originated from the gods, regardless of whatever form or name you call them by.

Creating a Prayer to the Divine Self

In general there are five steps to creating a prayer. You can find more information about writing prayers for deity in my book *Dedicant, Devotee, Priest*. Here, I have altered the steps for the purpose of honoring our own divine spark.

Writing prayer is kind of like dialing a phone number or putting coordinates into the Stargate. You want to be specific about the

energy or divinity you are calling on. If you dial the wrong number or put in the wrong coordinates, you aren't going to end up where you want to be. Dialing the wrong number spiritually can lead to all sorts of issues. When it involves spirits, it could mean you attract the wrong entity or aspect of a deity. Just as the gods are multifaceted, so too are we. There are many layers to our own spiritual and psychological make up. We go by many names and titles, ranging from describing our relationships with others to the magical names we take on to the nicknames only our friends use for us. When we seek to connect to the Divine within, we are seeking to connect to our higher selves, rather than our ego or shadow selves, where our doubts and insecurities live. The creation of this prayer should come from an honest place within ourselves. It is meant to acknowledge ourselves as we are and reaffirm that we are part of the sacred.

The first step is to identify ourselves. This can be saying your name or names, if you wish to include the magical ones you use. It can also be naming your characteristics and relationships to others that define you. Step two is acknowledging things you have done or achieved. Picking big breakthrough moments or things you are proud of would be appropriate. Step three is naming your relationship with the spiritual world. Perhaps you are a priest or priestess of a certain deity or a devotee of a certain tradition or spiritual being. It can also be a simple acknowledgment that a piece of the Divine resides within you. Step four is petitioning or giving thanks. This can be giving gratitude for the things you have in your life. It can be an affirmation that you wish to see yourself in a more positive light, a statement of body positivity, or offering forgiveness to yourself. We are often our own worst critics, and sometimes offering ourselves forgiveness for the things we feel we have messed up on in our lives can be a powerful thing.

1. Call out to the inner Divine.
   a. Identify yourself by name, titles, characteristics.
   b. Identify relationships, e.g., "husband of ___," "daughter of ___," etc.
   c. Establish that you wish to honor the sacred within yourself.
2. Praise your deeds and accomplishments.
   a. Name the things you are proud of achieving, no matter how big or small you feel they are.
   b. What are the things you have overcome?
3. State agreements and relationships between you and the Divine.
   a. Name a relationship with a deity/spirit/spiritual path you practice.
   b. Acknowledge that the sacred is both within and without.
   c. Name any titles you hold in your spiritual path: priest/ess, Witch, etc.
4. Requests, petitions, and thanking.
   a. Forgive yourself.
   b. Affirmation of self-love, body positivity, etc.
   c. Give yourself permission to do things for yourself.
   d. Give gratitude for your life and the things and people in it.
   e. Or all the above.

Honoring the Divine Self

The idea that the divine essence within us is the breath of a goddess or god resonates with me. We interact and experience the world around us through breath. Breathing in the scent of your favorite incense or the smell of fresh-baked cookies can alter our mood and energies almost instantly. Prayer also involves breath, and as Witches, we know words have power. This makes intentional breath work and intentional speech fundamental magical practices.

Once you have written your prayer, the next step is to use it. Approaching the process as a magical act is key. Before saying your prayer aloud, spend some time grounding and centering. Take several deep breaths in, and as you do, you might want to meditate on the idea of the sacred breath that animates life and bestows a spark of the Divine within us. There are several breathing techniques you can use, including fourfold breath. Fourfold breath, or box breathing, is inhaling to the count of four, holding your breath to the count of four, exhaling to the count of four, then holding your lungs empty to the count of four. Use whatever technique you are most comfortable with.

When you feel centered and ready to begin, spend a few moments connecting to your higher self. What does that self look like? What does that spark of the Divine within look like? Is it a certain color or shape? Do you see it as an inner flame or something else? Let that image grow and become sharper. See that image overlapping with your physical form and shining brightly from within you. When you are ready, say the prayer that you have written.

Ideally, try to make this a regular practice. You may be surprised with the results you get and how it might influence your day. Even more importantly, you may see how it alters your view of yourself. The world can be harsh. Letting our divine spark shine more brightly can make all the difference in navigating our way through life and finding that the Divine is no further away than our own hearts.

Resources

Crawford, Jackson, trans. and ed. *The Poetic Edda: Stories of the Norse Gods and Heroes.* Indianapolis, IN: Hackett Publishing, 2015.

Leet, Leonora. *The Secret Doctrine of the Kabbalah: Recovering the Key to Hebraic Sacred Science.* Rochester, VT: Inner Traditions, 1999.

Fire Dance Magic

Astrea Taylor

Our ancestors revered fire, and on special occasions, they combined it with dancing. This ancient magical practice helped them celebrate transformations of all kinds, including seasonal markers such as Beltane and life changes like marriages. It was very likely used in personal magic too. I believe fire dancing is a wonderful and transformative activity that anyone can do.

I have many years of experience dancing around a bonfire, and I'm also a professional fire dancer. I've swung poi, fire fans, and a fire umbrella. I've even hooped with it. With all my years of fire dancing, I've learned a lot about the magical aspects of it. In this article, I share some of my insights and I invite you to fire dance with me—safely, of course. Fire toys aren't for everyone, but if you can make a bonfire or light a few candles, you can dance with fire and enjoy this marvelous magic too. Before you grab your favorite lighter, read this article until the end for some important tips on magic and fire safety.

Prepare

With fire, safety always comes first. You must make sure the conditions are safe before lighting up. Think of this as the first step in successful fire dancing magic.

For a bonfire, prepare an area outdoors so nothing flammable is nearby, including dry leaves, dried grass, matches, lighters, or additional wood. Clear any items above and around the fire area (unless you plan on using a cauldron—see page 203). If it's too dry, windy, or bright, it's likely not safe to have a bonfire. You should probably delay until you can do it during a more favorable time. A good alternative is dancing with candles indoors.

For fire dancing with candles, locate a safe place for the candles to burn. They should be away from drafty areas like vents, windows, and fans. Use candleholders and remove anything hanging above the candles. Set the candles at least three inches away from each other and the wall and at least two foot from away from any flammable items, such as curtains. Consider placing the candles on a sturdy table in the middle of a cleared room so you can dance around them.

Purify

It's a good idea to cleanse before doing fire dance magic, as with any magical practice. Bathe and use incense or burning herbs to cleanse yourself and the space. Dress appropriately: long or droopy sleeves are not a good idea. You should also skip wearing silk or synthetic materials like polyester if you'll be near a bonfire. Consider tying back your hair if it's longer than your ears.

When everything is in place, play some music. Ideally, it will either allow you to cultivate a meditative mindset, or it will make you feel like dancing.

Spark

Before lighting up, craft an intention about your magical practice. Your intention should be something you can put energy toward with your dancing and the fire. Once you have a suitable intention, imagine it's a flickering flame in your heart. Take a few deep breaths to stoke your inner heart fire. When your chest feels warm and expansive, ignite your bonfire or your candles. Take a moment to watch the fire and honor the raw element.

Warm Up

Gaze at the fire and allow it to melt away any resistance to the dance. Let the fire and the music inspire movement in your body. If you wish, you could gently sway as you warm up and take up more space in your body. You can also try to mirror the motion of the dancing flames with your body. The important thing to remember is that your movement doesn't have to look amazing. It's more about letting the fire and the music shift the energy within you.

This is a great time to use the warmth of the fire to welcome your ancestors, spirits, or deities to participate in your magic. Simply call upon them and ask them to assist. Imagine they're dancing along with you.

Dance the Magic

After you're warmed up, start to incorporate a little magic into your fire dance. There are several options you can try, but the simplest method is to gaze at the fire and dance while speaking your spell or your intentions. It might take effort to join your spell and your steps, but try to do so.

If you can dance in a circle around your fire, you can cast a circle as you dance. Move in a clockwise circle to work toward a goal, or dance counterclockwise to decrease something's energy. For example, if you wish to attract a new friend, you could dance clockwise to increase the attraction aspect, or you could dance counterclockwise to banish your shyness.

If your spell or ritual isn't conducive to constant dancing, take a break to do whatever needs to be done.

Raise Energy

Fire dancing is a great way to raise energy. Our magical practices aways benefit whenever we do this. It gives us more energy to work with, which makes our magic stronger and more well-connected. To raise energy by fire dancing, increase the pace on your dance and spoken intention (as in the previous step). Ramp up your speed until you find a rhythm that matches the energy of your intention. Maintain the tempo and let your fire dancing boost your magic to the next level. When you feel you've reached a peak, release your intention up and away from you. Imagine it traveling along the fire smoke to reach its intended destination.

Escalate Your Ongoing Magic

Fire dancing is a great way to improve any of your ongoing magical workings too. Simply raise energy, think of your spells in progress, and send energy to them. You can use your original intentions or you can make new intentions. If you make new intentions, consider the Moon phase (waxing or waning), and think about the current stage of your goals and what would serve them best.

Burn Away Obstacles

Fire dancing is a great way to remove any obstacles that stand in the way of your intentions. To do this, feel your internal impediments while you're dancing. You may wish to exaggerate your dancing by stomping your feet or singing along. When you're in touch with what's blocking you internally, use your hands to make sweeping movements over your head and your body to wipe the stagnant energy away from you. With a conscious effort, push that energy toward the fire. Allow the blockages to burn up completely in the flames. Repeat these actions until you feel you've removed all the obstructions from yourself.

Next, clear away any energetic connections you may have with obstacles that exist outside of you. These may feel like slight catches in the air or connections that you need to sever. Extend your hands away from your body and sweep the external obstacles toward the fire. Throw them all into the fire. Continue until you feel that all your external blocks are gone.

This practice could be a sole magical activity, or you could consider bringing in new energy afterward with a spell or a ritual.

Use a Cauldron

If you're making a potion, you may want to use a cauldron over the fire. The easiest way to do this is with a metal tripod designed for cauldrons. One of the best things about dancing around a fire with a cauldron is that it warms the ingredients up in more ways than one. You're not only adding heat from the fire, but you're also giving your spiral energy to it as well.

You'll need to set it up before lighting the fire to avoid burning yourself. You'll also need to watch the contents. Use fireproof mitts and equipment so you don't burn yourself on the metal or the potion.

Trance

You can also let your mind travel on a different wavelength with some fire trance. Many people who have trouble meditating find that it's easier when they can focus on a mesmerizing fire. If you've never tried it, it's worth giving it a shot.

For fire trance, first get comfortable. You can stand and dance, or sit still or sway if you'd prefer. Gaze into the flames and breathe deeply. Allow the fire to release any thoughts. Enjoy the visual sensation of the flickering light. Focus on different parts of the fire and evaluate what that does to your trance state. Gazing at the bright blue flames can be a different experience compared to looking at the soft orb of light the fire emits. If you're certain you won't get burned, get a little closer so the fire. Let it take up a larger field of your vision. Experiment and find the best visual for your trance state.

Additional Safety Tips

And now, here are a few commonsense tips:

• Don't leave a fire unattended.
• Keep kids and pets away from the fire.
• When it's time to extinguish the fire, do so thoroughly before leaving the area.
• Remember to hydrate, especially when you're done fire dancing. It's a great way to balance out all the fire energy.
• When your fire dance magic is done, consider eating a snack or a meal to nourish yourself.

Welsh Snakeskin Powder

Mhara Starling

Working with what the land provided and what was easily accessible seems to be a core principle found in folk magic across the world. The Welsh have a long history of folk magical traditions, and these traditions often made use of the virtuous gifts the natural landscape provided the people. Wales, the Celtic nation nestled in the western part of the British Isles, has a long tradition of folk magical specialists. The fact that in the native language of Wales, *Cymraeg*, we have a wide variety of terms to describe magical practitioners is proof of just how large a role magic played in Wales. *Swynydd, dynion/gwragedd hysbys, consuriwr,* and *gwiddan* are just a few examples of terms associated with those who were deeply knowledgeable and learned in the art of magic. The folk magical practitioners of Wales's past did not have access to occult or metaphysical stores that provided them with the tools and ingredients of their trade— no, they had to make do with what they could source themselves.

One thing utilized in a variety of Welsh magical practices was the shed skin of a snake. Snakes played a prominent role in Welsh folklore. It was believed that snakes would gather together in convocation at certain times of the year and, whilst hissing in unison, would create a mystical bubble that would harden into a *glain neidr*—a snake stone. A snake stone, depending on the source, is usually either a glassy bead-like object, often with a hole through the center, or it is a hag stone, a stone with a natural hole in it. Serpents in general were considered intelligent, cunning creatures to the Welsh. One of the most notorious snakes native to Wales is the adder, a small snake with a zigzag pattern that decorates its back. The adder is the only venomous snake in Wales and due to this has quite the reputation. Having grown up in a rural, coastal part of Wales, I knew quite a few people who had suffered the bite of an adder. My mother was always cautioning us to watch where we step and to

keep an eye out for a snake with a black diamond or zigzag pattern. Numerous old folk beliefs that claim to keep the adder and its bite away, but it must have also been considered rather fortuitous to stumble upon the shed skin of an adder. The shed remains of a snake's skin in general were utilized in various magical practices, but the skin of an adder was the most sought after.

In 1887, the Welsh priest Elias Owen presented an essay at the *Eisteddfod,* a Welsh cultural festival, that won him a silver medal. This essay was an exploration of Welsh folklore, customs, and old beliefs. In this essay, Owen outlines the methods in which snakeskin was utilized in traditional Welsh magic. According to Owen, snakeskin could be used to heal wounds and illnesses, predict the future, make people confident and strong both physically and mentally, and unveil any lies, among many other things.

As a *Swynwraig,* a Welsh folk Witch, I have over the years utilized the knowledge collected by Owen and other folklorists and historians and experimented with using snakeskin in various powders. I have found the powders I have created using snakeskin to be exceptionally effective and highly useful. Through my experimentation, I came to the realization that using snakeskin that I had found along the sandy dunes and coastal paths that surrounded the village I come from made my workings much more effective than, say, had I used the skin of my brother's pet snake, which he gave to me. However, even the powders I created with the snakeskin provided by my brother worked very well—therefore, if you have a pet snake, this may be the perfect magical method of utilizing the skin your scaly friend naturally sheds.

Base Snakeskin Powder

Here, I will outline the method of making the base snakeskin powder, which can be used alone for a variety of uses. I will also share some additional recipes for powders with a specific purpose.

You will need:
Shed skin of a snake
Scissors
Outdoor space where you can safely burn things
Lighter
Fireproof bowl
Tongs or something to handle very hot things with
Pestle or other grinding tool

Gather your collected snakeskin. The amount that you will need depends on how much of the powder you wish to create. Cut the skin into sheets that are approximately 2 to 3 inches in length.

Consider the timing best suited to creating this powder. If planetary timings are important to your practice, perhaps you might choose to create this base powder on a Tuesday, under the guidance of the planet Mars, drawing forth Mars's empowering and fiery qualities. Similarly, if you work closely with the Moon, it may be best to create this powder during the Full Moon or when the Moon is waxing. This all depends on how you personally work, though I have found that this powder's efficacy is only heightened when the movement of the celestial bodies and the virtues of the days of the week are taken into consideration.

Take yourself outdoors to a place where it will be safe for you to use fire. Ideally, you will place your firesafe bowl on a stone surface. Also ensure you are not wearing flammable clothing. Set up your tools at the ready and have your sheets of snakeskin in a jar or bowl nearby.

One sheet at a time, you will now use your tongs to hold the snakeskin over your bowl. Light the sheet on fire and drop it into your bowl. You may need to re-light the skin a few times to ensure it is fully burnt. You may also need to move the skin around in the bowl to stop it from sticking to the bottom. The skin needs to turn into a black, clumpy, ash-like substance. Repeat this step until you have burnt all your snakeskin and all you have left are the black clumps in your bowl.

Once the snakeskin and the bowl have cooled down, take your pestle or grinding tool and begin grinding the charred skin into a fine powder. When the whole snakeskin has been ground into an ashy, black powder, it is now ready to be used as a base powder. You can choose to either place this powder into a jar now or continue to create a powder blend.

Uses for Base Snakeskin Powder

What can you use this base powder for and how? This base powder will empower you and alleviate any bouts of low self-esteem. Place some of this powder in your shoe, and it will boost your confidence as well as allow you to be noticed and fully appreciated by those around you—very useful before an important meeting, a date, or an event you are nervous about.

Recite these words aloud before sprinkling the powder into your shoe, as a focus for your intended purpose:

Skin of snake, stir my spirit.
Let me be without fear this day.
Cast away doubt; neutralize and clear it.
Allow me to be the me I wish to portray.

Sprinkling this powder upon the clothes of another will also ensure they cannot lie to you. Spreading some at your doorstep is a way of protecting your home from any ill intention.

Snakeskin Powder Blends

I like to add other herbal ingredients into the ashy snakeskin powder in order to achieve other goals and desires. Here are a few examples of things you could add to the snakeskin powder and what it might then be used for with those additions. These are examples from my very own *llyfrau cyfrin,* magical journals.

To Receive Messages, Guidance, or Visions of the Future in Your Dreams

Add 2 teaspoons of lavender, 2 teaspoons of mugwort, and 1 drop of dragon's blood oil to 4 teaspoons of the snakeskin powder. Mix and grind well, adding dry ingredients first and only adding the drop of oil in last. Place the powder you have created into a small white or black pouch. Place this under your pillow. This powder is best created on a Monday, on a Full Moon, or both. Draw upon the power of the Moon to fulfill your desire and bring about interesting dreams.

To Offer You Protection from Any Ill Wishes

Add 3 teaspoons of rosemary to 3 teaspoons of the snakeskin powder and mix well. Add a handful of dried rowan berries or the ground twigs of a rowan branch. Place a little of this mixture into a small red pouch. Write on a piece of paper these words: *Melltithion yn ôl at unrhyw un a ddymuna unrhyw casineb yn erbyn fi. Dwi o dan ofal ysbryd yr sarffes, y criafol, a'r rhosmari* (I send back the curses of those who wish me ill. I am under the care of the spirit of the serpent, the rowan, and the rosemary). Roll up or fold the piece of paper and place it in the pouch. Carry this pouch with you at all times or wear it around your neck on a red cord for potent protection. It is best to create this protective charm on a Tuesday, the day of Mars, drawing forth Mars's virtues of defense and strength.

To Attract Love and Recognition

Mix 2 teaspoons of the snakeskin powder with 2 teaspoons of rose petals and 1 teaspoon of sugar. Mix these ingredients well. Every Friday night, fill a bowl with warm water and pour some of the mixture into the water. Wash your hands in the water whilst visualizing what it is you wish to achieve, whether it is love, friendship, or recognition that you wish to manifest into your life. If a Full Moon falls on a Friday, do this outdoors whilst looking up at the Moon's face. Smell the scent of the mixture in the water and allow the spirit of the serpent and the virtues of the rose and sugar to bring forth the good blessings you desire.

The Spirit of the Serpent

The beauty of the snakeskin powder lies in its multipurpose nature. I have found that adding the powdered snakeskin into practically any magical powder or sprinkling a little about my ritual space acts as an amplifier for my workings.

An old Welsh word for a serpent was *sarffes*, and the nature of the snake itself is symbolic of the very energetic flow that connects all things. Specifically, the snake symbolizes the ebb and flow of the Earth's energies. Drawing forth on the potency and folkloric legacy of the snake is deeply powerful and magical. The serpent or snake is a creature that has long been misunderstood, demonized, feared and scorned, but those of us with a magical inclination tend to have a soft spot for the unloved and misunderstood. Perhaps the snake is not only symbolic of the ebb and flow of the Earth's magic but also a potent emblem or symbol for those of us who do not fit the mold society wishes we would. There is much that can be learned from the snake. The snake is a powerful and enigmatic spiritual and magical ally, and understanding that the skin it sheds and leaves behind carries with it the memories of a fraction of a life lived in tune with the land enables us to connect with the spirit of the serpent.

A Call to the Spirit of the Snake

Cyfarchaf i ysbryd y neidr, y sarffes.
Rho aed i mi, i ddeall cyfrinachau'r byd naturiol.
Rho aed i mi yn fy doethgrefft, fy swyngyfaredd, fy, ysbrydiaeth,
    ac ysbrydoliaeth.

I call to the spirit of the snake, the serpent.
Aid me in understanding the hidden secrets of the natural world.
Aid me in my Witchcraft, my magic, my spirituality, and inspiration.

Resources

Owen, Elias. *Welsh Folk-Lore: A Collection of Folk-Tales and Legends of North Wales.* Oswestry, UK: Woodall, Minshall, and Co., 1896.

Sikes, Wirt. *British Goblins: Welsh Folk-Lore, Fairy Mythology, Legends and Traditions.* London: Sampson Low, Marston, Searle & Rivington, 1880.

The Magick in Our Hands

Vernon Mahabal

The expression "Life does not come with instructions" is not a conviction subscribed to by palmists. Rather, readers of the hand view the study of the palm as the foremost science of self-realization.

My journey on the path of palmistry began when I was seventeen. There, on the shelf of my high school library, was a slim volume on hand reading. Although quite distinct from anything I'd before encountered, I was very drawn to it. Though raised in an empty vacuum of mechanistic atheism, I nonetheless felt a firm innervation that this was something genuine and sagacious. Its contents were my first initiation into the enchanting world of metaphysics. Carrying it around, I'd look at my friends' hands and sometimes make notes. Of course, they told me I was crazy and should just stick to baseball. Nonetheless, I persisted. I knew there was something to it.

After graduating, I continued to read hands and acquire palmistry tomes, but my discipline was scattered and unfocused. Having read the Bhagavad Gita, I joined the Vedic society founded by Swami Prabhupada and lived a monastic ashram life for five years. I became immersed in the mystical arts of the Indian subcontinent, the recitation of ancient mantras, and the study of Oriental (Sidereal) cosmology. I became conversant with Sanskrit and traveled to India many times. It was an exhilarant life.

Not long after leaving the ashram, I would meet the person who would become my palmistry mentor. There was always a queue waiting for Patrick as he set up his table on St. Mark's Place in NYC. I spent four years watching him give readings and taking everything in. There was usually a lesson after each reading! Known popularly as the Magick Warrior, Patrick gave lectures on Western

mysticism and ceremonial magick, which attracted a who's who of Manhattan's Pagan and Wiccan community. Additionally, he was a popular soothsayer among NYC's flourishing punk/metal scene, reading for fans and musicians alike.

Patrick versed me in the hand's astrological overlay and stressed its true eminence as a magickal tool and not to neglect the intuitive over the "scientific." This was difficult for me to work with at the time, as I wasn't yet "there" psychically. However, as my skills and experience grew, I was able to incorporate and value this very intrinsic feature of hand analysis.

Follow Your Heart

I'm often asked, "What if you see something bad on a person's hands—do you tell them?" "Bad" often refers to accidents, health issues, or untimely death. These are certainly seen, and if a danger can be averted, I won't hesitate to address it. However, I have a different take on what I see as bad in the hand. What's seen more frequently, and is just as challenging, is a person who is in the wrong career, living with the wrong partner, or residing in an unpropitious location. I see this misalignment in almost every hand. Roughly 20 percent or less of all those I read for are presentably engaged in their right life work. Of course, it is my job to properly position people—but to me, this state of affairs does not speak of a population healthily pursuing their life calling.

Not having the discrimination to recognize that spiritual forces are the generating principle behind all material expansion, our institutions teach us to identify ourselves as a product of the material rather than the spiritual. We then become consumed by the logistical instead of the limitless.

It's a common occurrence that at some point during the reading, I will state to my client who, let's say, has been in marketing for twenty years that "your natural propensity is to be within architectural or structural design." One hundred percent of the time they will reply, "Well, yes, that's exactly what I wanted to pursue after high school, but my parents or the school counselor talked me out

of it!" We are not brought up to trust the still small voice within. We consequently resort to traversing a conventional career course, which only causes us to miss out on ascending to our own personal greatness. The message in our hands exclaims, "Trust your heart! Your heart will never lie."

I'm often in awe of the phenomenal attributes displayed upon hands—yet I may maintain some skepticism that my client will deliciously milk it. I encourage all I can, to not in any way minimize the power and capability within. "What the mind can conceive, one can achieve" is a statement I am prone to invoke. And if there is one group that truly recognizes and embraces this aphorism, it is our Pagan and Wiccan community. The boundless expanse of consciousness and the importance of mental discipline are acknowledged by all those engaged in metaphysical and spiritual development. It may be up to us, and us only, to elevate human consciousness.

You may have the experience of holding your open palms slightly above another's and feeling a very real sensation. Sometimes it feels warm. It can also feel a touch magnetic. This energy is the frequency of the subconscious. A seasoned palmist can secure the entirety of this subconscious bandwidth by way of clairaudience or clairsentience (psychic hearing and feeling). Consequently, a palmist can know much about the influence and impact the bearer has upon their environment—things like their degree of power, fame, and status and even the scale of their avarice or empathy toward others. The transference of this efficacious current is in constant subliminal operation—without us being aware. Of course, this conduction is a two-way street, but the "stronger" or "senior" person in the relationship is always likely to predominate. Taking all this into account, this is why it's so important to choose wisely regarding our acquaintances. This pulsating frequency of the subconscious body is fully replicated upon the palm and open to be accessed by the reader. This is another wonderful aspect of the magick in our hands.

The Heart in Our Hands

Now let's look at our own hands. When expressing your emotions, are you British or Italian? Take notice of the horizontal line traversing an inch below the fingers. Commonly termed the "heart line," this crease is more correctly the fourth or heart chakra line. (Each of the seven major chakras are represented upon our hands in the form of lines.) Beginning from the pinky side and ending its journey either under the middle or index finger, it discloses our temper of emotional expression. For this exercise, look at this line on your right hand (left-handed people included). Eschewing its length, observe whether it courses a straight path throughout or ends with an upward curve toward the fingers.

Your Fourth Chakra Line Curves Up

This means that you are very much in touch with the feelings within your heart and can express them when required. And in situations

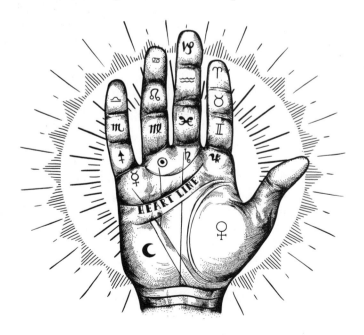

where you are prevented or are not comfortable to share them, you become disheartened and even frustrated. You are in love with love and are most happy to be in a reciprocal relationship of closeness and intimacy. On the downside, because you are an idealistic romantic, you may have experienced more than a few relationships of being taken advantage of. So stand your ground and keep your radar up.

In the magickal department, you feel empowered when your prayers and incantations are spoken boldly and vibrantly. You enjoy the pomp and formality of a well-ordered ceremonial undertaking. Magick also comes alive for you within a celebratory group setting with colorful fashion, opulent tools, and lots of candles and incense included. Your Book of Shadows is also very elegant, employing various colors of ink, drawings, and photos.

You Possess a Predominantly Straight Fourth Chakra

Your feelings may run very deep, but you have difficulty expressing them. Talking about your ideas and views may be easy, but not when it comes to sharing your feelings. In relationships, you are emotionally reserved and self-contained, and you may be accused of acting cool and aloof without intending to. You require a partner in life who will take the time to put you in a comfortable space when required so that you feel safe to share your feelings. Consequently, this straight fourth chakra line is often found on highly driven professionals. Emotion is there and it's usually transmuted over into one's career.

In magick, you may *prefer* to be the solitary practitioner! Your ceremonies are quiet and low-key, and you do much of the workings within your mind. Incantations are also said softly or internally. Despite this, your rituals can be quite powerful and effectual, as you are adept at focusing on your intentions.

The Mantra to the Stars

In Vedic cosmology, the arts of palmistry and astrology are called *jyotish*. A Sanskrit word, jyotish literally means the "divine science

of the stars." For thousands of years, the jyotishi played a most respected and integral role in Vedic India. They read for all levels of monarchy and the various affairs of the citizens, both public and private. They even gave the name to the newborn child upon describing their nature and destiny to the parents. In the Vedic view, unlike much of the West, it is understood that the planets were created by the Divine Goddess and God, Lakshmi Narayan, as well as the great demigods. Therefore, their energy and influences within the universe are auspicious and beneficial.

For the society at large, the practice of jyotish was seen as essential for the progressive advancement of human culture. And for the individual, palmistry and astrology were used as a road map to chart one's advancement of consciousness for this life and the next. The jyotishi is trained to see the planets not as just gas or fire giants but as the dwelling places of the great demigods. In fact, in Vedic astrology, the "houses" are actually their places of residence. A palmist or astrologer is taught to have an actual relationship with these universal managers and to petition them to release their wisdom when doing a reading for a client. Everything is personal. The higher universal agents are to be seen as friendly and favorable.

In this regard, the jyotishi must view themselves as a transparent *via media*—from heaven to Earth—a true messenger. Therefore, a humble prayer to petition these planetary gods to bestow their knowledge always commences the work of the diviner. Any prayer asking for grace and benediction is most helpful to our practice. Thousands of years ago, the great seers and soothsayers of ancient India bestowed the following mantra (incantation) to this planet. It is the most powerful prayer for astral connection. And if uttered before a consultation, it can give the power of *trikala-jna* (the knowledge of past, present, and future). There is no more spotless prayer for the reader of the stars. It can be said aloud or under one's breath. It is an incantation that especially draws down planetary consciousness but can also be employed in other

forms of divination. The great palmists, astrologers, and seers of India always had this mantra on their lips:

Om Namo Bhagavate Vasudevaya

Our own two hands are magickal tools. The following exercises will summon forth our innate psychical gifts.

Ritual for Intuition

When looking for clarity, and logic and reason have failed to slake, it's time to consult your intuition. The following practice is most natural, soothing, and remarkably effective. Escape to a quiet place, take a few breaths, and close your eyes. (You may do this standing up or sitting down.) With a mood of trustful expectancy, place your left hand firmly upon your heart. Keep a slight space between your fingers. The left hand embodies our feminine and emotional nature—exactly as our hearts. Now imagine your hand and heart to be

one, and feel all vitality in your being converging upon this zone. Stay centered in this meditation for a few minutes, while asking your questions. Do not try to empty the mind of thoughts; rather, continue to petition the heart for its intuition. And very soon, you'll receive your answer. Your answer will be most assuring and most satisfying.

Ritual for Calm and Balance

If you are experiencing a strong bout of stress and anxiety and wish to return to composure, sit down comfortably and clasp your hands together. Hold them in this position for a few minutes while taking some solid breaths. Now focus attentively upon the stresses in your heart and visualize this negative energy transferring into your hands. You'll feel them becoming a bit warm. Almost instantly you'll feel relaxed and centered and ready to move forward comfortably. Our right hand contains the information held within our left brain, and our left hand comprises all that is in our right brain. Our empirical left brain is the repository of logic and reason. And our right brain by comparison is the spiritual storehouse of dreams, imagination, and intuition. They could not be more opposite. When two hands are joined together, it orchestrates a synthesis of harmony and balance, stimulating decided mental equilibrium.

Ritual for Inspiration

Are you lacking inspiration or just seeking the way forward? Go outdoors and try this simple ceremony. Standing up and keeping a bit of distance between your feet, raise your hands above your head. Hold your palms open and face them toward the sky. Every planet in this universe emits its own distinctive band of frequency, and the cosmos is a symphony of celestial vibration. Imagine your palm and fingers to be like radars, taking in these planetary pulsations. Our eternal, spiritual soul working through the agency of the hand takes in those specific frequencies we require and remains indifferent to those we do not. Feeling part and parcel with these galactic energies, go ahead and ask for a message to be given. Be

hopeful and receptive as you ask for support and direction. Our palms are always taking in frequencies as leaves with sunlight, but holding them up to the sky—with intention—ensures a banquet of celestial nourishment. Palms held to the sky during the day, or toward the Sun, inspire motivations in the direction of practical achievements. Held to the nighttime sky, especially toward the Moon, palms inspire spiritual or devotional directions. Two, possibly three, minutes spent in this ritual is perfectly sufficient.

This simple ceremony can connect us with higher benevolent forces, providing the enthusiasm to catalyze a topical affair or, more importantly, inspire a great purpose. Our advanced predecessors, who knew their relationship with the stars, were well familiar with this ritual, and it's frequently encountered in Egyptian art. Reach for the sky!

Water Magic

Palm Tree Magic

Natalie Zaman

There's something about traveling by car (or foot or bike) that really makes a trip magical. Aerial views have their charm, but watching the landscape evolve, subtly or abruptly, as you pass through it is a wonder. I once watched a field of saguaro cactuses morph into pine trees as we drove up a mountain and the elevation of the land changed. Once while driving westward, I saw a cloud that turned out to be the snow-capped peak of Mount Rainier. This is how I experienced my first palm tree—from the ground.

My first trip to Florida was by car. We were driving down I-95, that ubiquitous highway that runs inland down the east coast—not nearly as interesting, but much faster that Route 1. When we got to Georgia, I saw them, standing tall in the median of the highway: bushy-topped (probably) cabbage palms. Gorgeous! (Note: Palm trees have been creeping northward for some time and can be found in nature north of the Georgia border, but this was my first experience of seeing a palm tree "in the wild.")

Palm trees conjure up vistas of tropical beaches, steamy forests, and fig-laden desert oases, perhaps shading tiled, splashing fountains. Palm trees have always had a hand in magic—bad pun absolutely intended. Palm trees are called palms because their long-fronded leaves resemble a palm and fingers—but it should be noted that not all palms have fronds. Palms are "human trees," as the average palm has the same life span as a human (seventy to eighty years, with some varieties living over a hundred). They are fast growing and don't produce rings, so there is debate whether or not the palm is actually a tree.

Science says that palms are angiosperms—flowering plants with a single stalk. Whatever you think a palm may be, there is definitely great variety; there are over 2,500 species of palm trees and shrubs, and they usually fall into two categories: pinnate (the type that has feathery fronds) and palmate (the type that has wide, broad leaves). Generally, you'll find palms in warm climates, but there are palms that can survive even if temperatures get into the teens!

Like all natural beings—especially trees—palms have their own special brand of magic and each variety has particular attributes to offer. There are many great resources for finding out the magical properties of trees, including tropical ones. While I would certainly turn to these when incorporating a particular tree into your practice, I encourage you to observe the tree yourself. I'm not suggesting that you make up magical attributes, but drawing on the tree's physical nature—its growth patterns, produce, and life cycle—will tell you much about what it's capable of esoterically. For example, a fruiting palm like a date palm would be good for uplifting, energy-raising magic (dates = sugar = energy!). What does the tree look like? The triangle palm—one of my favorites—resembles a peacock with its tail feathers out. The broad leaves on this palm grow outward (left to right) and upward from a central stalk. This observation tells me that this palm would be good for workings dealing with confidence. Perhaps you'd plant this palm in your front garden to draw beauty, majesty, and success into your home.

Don't forget to take your personal experience with a tree into consideration! Getting zonked on the head by an acorn when I was at a Renaissance fair colored my experience of oaks for a while. It was hot, and I was moody and literally steaming when it happened. The "sweat" dripping into my eye turned out to be blood, so a stop at a first aid station was a necessity. At first I was angry, but the incident made me sit, get a drink and cool off—lesson learned. That being said, you do *not* want to get tapped in a similar way by a coconut! A full-size coconut weighs between three and five pounds, and a coconut tree can soar up to a hundred feet into the sky. The weight times the distance of a falling coconut equals something terrible—do not linger under coconut trees! But to return to personal experience with palm trees, let's look at our friend, the date palm again:

My own history with the date palm goes back to my childhood, and my first experiences with ritual. I grew up in a Catholic house where preparation for Easter began with Ash Wednesday. Ash Wednesday's ashes are made from the fronds of the date palm— the same given out a few weeks later on Palm Sunday, the day that Jesus arrived in Jerusalem, fulfilling the prophecy of Zechariah. On this occasion, folks lined the road with palm fronds or waived them as Jesus passed by. In this way, the palm plays much the same role as the laurel (i.e., a laurel wreath denoting victory and accomplishment). The ashes of the palm are a reminder of human mortality— and the immortality of the soul. I've carried this meaning of the palm into my practices today (as you will see in the vibrant palm smoothie!).

How can you incorporate palm trees and the gifts they bring into your magical practice? I love practical workings that are experiential and consumable.

Coconut Moon Water

When I first read about Keiko's "Power Wish" method for harnessing the energy of the Full and New Moons (must read!), I was delighted that she included a ritual for making Moon water in her book. This tool allows you to continue to tap into the power of a Full or New Moon days after the phase has passed. Keiko uses blue bottles or glasses to hold the water that catches the Moon's rays . . . but what if that water was *coconut* water?

Coconuts make their own "water," which immediately associates them with the water element. Their round shape and white flesh connect them to the Moon and therefore the Goddess. In fact, coconuts are self-contained wombs and perfect for incubation and birthing magic—what New and Full Moons are all about!

The liquid inside a fresh young coconut is a bit cloudy and has a subtle hint of coconut flavor. Like water, it's hydrating, but it also delivers a shot of calcium, magnesium, and potassium. (Be careful if you have issues with high potassium levels!) Coconut water is liquid coconut flesh—as the seed matures, the flesh gets thicker, and the liquid reduces. A young coconut will have more "water" in it than one that has been ripening for a while.

To make coconut Moon water, all you'll need is a coconut, a permanent marker, and a glass. (You can use clear glasses or blue ones like Keiko.) At the New or Full Moon, make sure to set your intention (New Moon) or statement of gratitude (Full Moon), then write it on the outside of your coconut. Open the coconut and pour its water into a glass to expose it to the Moon's phase. You can also keep the water in the coconut, but it's probably easier to strain it into a glass. Because you're not working with regular water, allow the Moon to touch the coconut water for an hour before drinking it. (Coconut water will only keep for a couple of days—and only if its kept cold!) When this simple ritual is complete, remember to use *all* of the coconut: harvest the flesh to incorporate into other magical works and recipes, and use the shell as a planter, compost, or fuel for a ritual fire.

How to Open a Coconut

I suggested earlier that palm trees are "human" trees—and the coconut is a reflection of that. The three depressions in a coconut's brown shell can resemble a face. (A fresh coconut right off the tree has a fibrous, green outer coat.) Use these depressions to access the water inside a coconut. If you don't have a drill handy, carefully and slowly use a wine corkscrew to bore into the coconut at each depression in the shell. You'll be able to feel when you've hit coconut flesh. Once you've "opened" all three holes, pour the water inside the coconut into a glass or a bowl, using a strainer to catch any loose pieces of coconut flesh and shell.

Oasis Candle

We've all been in the desert. Literal deserts are beautiful, but I'm talking about that barren place where you're drained of energy and weary from whatever journey you've been on, whether it's a project for work, a particularly trying week, or just a challenging experience. You need a moment to rest . . . and then, you see it. Somewhere ahead—you're not sure how far—it shimmers, beckoning: an oasis. I love the oasis of film and fiction. A lush green patch, shaded with palms, filled with fountains, figs, camels, tents, caftans, and magic carpets.

Real desert oases are not too far off this mark: made fertile by sometimes hidden sources of water, they are usually populated, planted (good farming land is hard to find in a desert!), and carefully maintained. In places like the Sahara, oases were often stops for trade routes. You may not live in or near a desert, but when you need a break, use this candle to conjure up the peace and relief an oasis has to offer.

I love working with beeswax sheets, as they are easy to manipulate, and the rolling up is a nice way to seal a spell! Blue and green are peaceful, hydrating colors; they represent the greenery and the water of the oasis. Because they induce peace, frankincense, sandalwood, and patchouli would be good choices of incense for this work.

You will need:
Incense in your favorite scent
1 square sheet of blue or green beeswax
Length of candle wicking that is at least 2 inches longer than the
   beeswax sheet
Palm or coconut oil
Sand or gold glitter

Light your incense, then lay the sheet of beeswax out on a flat surface. Place the wicking so that it is flush with one edge of the beeswax sheet and then press it into the wax. When you start rolling the candle, you will start at this end so that the wick will end up in the center of the candle. One end of the wick should be flush with the sheet—this will be the bottom of the candle. The other end should extend past the opposite edge.

Pour the coconut or palm oil onto a plate and dip your fingers in it. Using your fingers, write the words *rest, refresh,* and *peace* over and over onto the beeswax sheet with the oil. As you do so, visualize yourself at rest in an oasis. Feel the cool breeze over your face. See the palms waving above you. Smell the scent of incense and ripening fruit in the air.

When you feel that you have imbued the wax with these energies, sprinkle the gold glitter or sand (or both!) over the sheet with this blessing:

A spot of green in golden sand.
Restful, refreshing peace in hand!

Starting at the side with the wick, carefully roll the candle up, repeating the blessing. Carefully squeeze the candle so that the heat of your hands seals the layers of rolled beeswax together (if it's still loose, use a hairdryer to soften the wax, and then apply pressure to the seam to seal it shut.

Burn your oasis candle when you need a moment of refuge.

Vibrant Palm Smoothie

When I started spending a lot of time in South Florida, I found, much to my delight, that there was a smoothie shop nearly every five feet—and most of these tapped into the abundance of local, tropical produce to make their smoothies. One that I found myself drinking every day was a concoction called a "sunshine smoothie" for its sunny yellow color.

This recipe is inspired by my Florida fix. Creating it is a ritual, and its ingredients lift and lighten—the spices are also anti-inflammatory. It is a bit sweeter, with a little bite to it, and it uses the produce of four palm trees and plants. The coconut is restorative and nurturing, and if I was amazed by the sight of my first palm, I was absolutely dazzled the first time I actually saw bananas growing on a tree and not piled up in a bin at the supermarket! Bananas bring luck and prosperity. Among other magical properties, pineapples are symbols of welcome (hello, oasis!) and bring friendly vibes to this work. Is the pineapple a palm tree or shrub? There is some debate about this, but I'm swayed that its tropical tendencies, spiny skin, and spiky leaves hint of palmness. The last fruit in this smoothie, dates are called "the fruit of kings" and bring power and energy to the drink!

Make and drink this as a part of a ritual for refreshing the soul, restoring resiliency, or initiating the vibes for a sunny attitude.

You will need:
1½ cups coconut milk (plus a little more if needed)
1 banana
½ cup diced pineapple
1 medjool date

1 teaspoon "spiky spice mixture" (Mix together 1 tablespoon each powdered ginger, cinnamon, and black pepper with 2 tablespoons turmeric.)

Place each ingredient into a blender one at a time. As you do so, say this spell (or one of your own invention to invoke the power of the palm):

Fruit of the palm, bring warmth and light,
Refreshment, healing, and renewed sight!

Once all the ingredients are in the blender, process them until they're smooth. Add a little extra coconut milk if the mixture is too thick to drink through a straw. For a super chilly and refreshing smoothie, freeze the pineapple and banana before blending.

May the heart and hand of the palm bless you always and in all ways!

Resources

Keiko. *The Power Wish: Japan's Leading Astrologer Reveals the Moon's Secrets for Finding Success, Happiness, and the Favor of the Universe.* Translated by Reiko Yamanaka. New York: Penguin Life, 2020.

The Palm Identifier. www.palmidentifier.com. 2022.

Riffle, Robert Lee, Paul Craft, and Scott Zona. *The Encyclopedia of Cultivated Palms.* Portland, OR: Timber Press, 2003.

Von Martius, Karl Friedrich Philipp, and H. William Lack. *The Book of Palms.* Cologne, Germany: Taschen, 2017.

Whitehurst, Tess. *The Magic of Trees: A Guide to Their Sacred Wisdom & Metaphysical Properties.* Woodbury, MN: Llewellyn Publications, 2017.

The Flow State in Magic and Ritual

Lupa

*T*he night is cool, but the fire sparks hot enough for me to take a couple of steps back. Overhead, a three-quarter Moon casts silvery light. I breathe deeply and gently pick up my wolf skin cloak. Cradling her in my arms, I pace around the fire, bowing to it before raising the wolf skin to the sky. I continue around the fire, repeating this process again and again until everything has boiled down to: Night. Wolf. Fire. Blood in my veins.

I slip into the wolf skin and draw her head over my face. I feel her spirit wrap around me, shifting my energy to fur and tail and lengthen-

ing snout, where smell is more important than sight. We are together as one, and the fire lights our circling path. I begin to dance, channeling her energy through me into the ground below us and the air around us, allowing her to run again through my muscles and bones.

Nothing else matters. Nothing else exists but this moment and space. There are no other people here, no other beings, only: Night. Wolf. Fire. Blood in my veins.

What Is Flow?

Think of a time when you were so immersed in what you were doing that nothing could distract you. Everything else drifted away until all you noticed was the task at hand, and everything felt as though it was coming together perfectly. Perhaps you were creating a piece of art or writing; maybe you were dancing or going for a long run. Often musicians drop "into the groove," especially when playing harmoniously with others. Many of us have also experienced this state of mind during intense rituals like the one I described.

This is called a flow state. First described by Dr. Mihály Csíkszentmihályi, a Hungarian-American psychologist, flow is when you are completely immersed in an experience or task. It often feels like you are at your absolute best, bringing all your skill to the surface and nourishing fresh creativity. Unlike distraction or some forms of hyperfocus, this is a completely positive state that brings a deep feeling of emotional and mental satisfaction and leaves you refreshed and encouraged.

There are several components to the flow state:

- You are totally focused on what's happening right now.
- You have exceptionally keen focus on your actions.
- There's no hesitation, embarrassment, or self-consciousness.
- You have a deep need to create something amazing, the best you can possibly do.

- You feel completely in control of what you're doing, and you are at the peak of your skills.
- You can adapt easily as your needs and that of your activity shift and change.
- Time seems to disappear, and you no longer notice how it passes.
- You never want this experience to end—it's just that good!

Anyone has the potential to reach a flow state, though some people seem to drop into it more naturally than others. Creative people seem especially prone to flow, and it was artists who initially inspired Csíkszentmihályi to explore what they were experiencing when they were so engrossed in their work that they forgot to eat or sleep. Spiritual experiences across many religions also make use of this state, and it has often helped bond people together in a common focus or goal.

Many people who enter a flow state describe the experience as a sort of altered state of consciousness or reality. The term *flow*, in fact, came about as many people Csíkszentmihályi spoke with said it was like being carried along by a current of water (in an exhilarating, rather than terrifying, manner). Other people mention feeling as though they had left their bodies and were watching themselves in this activity. Some may experience the breakdown of their ego, as the boundaries between the self and the rest of the world dissolve. Even once they have come back to their normal state of mind, they may still experience the "high" of flow for some time afterward.

The Autotelic Self

Csíkszentmihályi described people who do things for their own sake, rather than for external rewards like power or money, as autotelic (*auto* means "self," while *telos* means "reward"—so, self-rewarding). They want to see their goal through to the end, and that completion is enough satisfaction for them. They are frequently very curious, creative people who are interested in how the world works. Often willing to push themselves to higher limits, they want to grow and become better, not to get better jobs or achieve fame, but simply because self-improvement is a reward in and of itself. And, perhaps most importantly, they feel that they have a great deal of control over their lives, even within the constraints of society, health, and other external factors.

In my personal (anecdotal) experience, Pagans and other magic users trend high toward autotelic personalities. It takes both curiosity and creativity to create ritual practices and enact them in meaningful ways. A high tolerance for challenge helps quite a bit, particularly when we are new and learning, or striving to new levels or areas of practice. The very practice of magic requires a belief that we can create change in our world in spite of the limitations we may be facing. And while we may have specific goals in mind when we create a spell or ritual, there is a joy we feel in the act itself, regardless of outcome.

How can you nourish and encourage your autotelic self? Here are a few suggestions:

- Remember what you did as a kid that made the hours pass by like minutes and that you would go back to anytime you were given the opportunity? If that's something you've put aside as an adult, it's time to rediscover it! You don't have to make it your main focus; just give yourself a corner of your life to rekindle that interest or activity and remember what that feeling is like.
- Engage your curiosity! Practice asking "why" and "how" questions and then finding the answers. One of the great things about smartphones, for example, is the fact that you can instantly look up just about anything, anywhere, anytime. So indulge yourself whenever you have one of those "I wonder . . ." questions pop into your head, even if you may have to wait a bit until you have the time to actually do your research.

- Get those creative juices flowing! You don't have to be a Really Great Artist™ in order to make great art, whether visual art, music, dance, or other creative activities. Give yourself permission to just create for its own sake, in whatever media you prefer. If you want to start with a beginner's kit, that's perfectly acceptable; so is jumping in with both feet and seeing what happens! What's important is that you're allowing yourself that time and space to create, regardless of the subjective quality of the outcome.
- Challenge yourself! Try something new or revisit something you haven't done in years. Maybe you want to explore a new recipe in the kitchen or expand your professional skills in a new direction. Perhaps there's an area of your spiritual practice that you've wanted to do more with, or a deity or spirit has indicated interest in working with you. Whatever it is, the point is to get out of your comfort zone and see what you're capable of.

While these and other practices are good for your autotelic self at any time, you may find them especially helpful if you've been feeling burned out, depressed, exhausted, or otherwise just not at your best. Don't go into it with the pressure of "I *must* make myself feel better" or "I *have* to do this because Lupa suggested it." Instead, if you happen to be in one or more of these states while you're working with your autotelic self, you may find that a side benefit is that you do in fact feel better!

As I'm writing this, I am myself working through a bad burnout period that has lasted for a couple of years. I got so focused on work as, well, *work* that I forgot to have fun as well. (It's pretty sad when someone who is a professional creative stops enjoying her daily activities!) I used some of the practices above, not to force myself out of burnout, but simply to give myself breaks from the daily grind. And it has worked—the more I allow myself time to explore and play, the more I rediscover the parts of me that were buried under years of stress and "adulting."

Flow State and Ritual

Improving your relationship with your autotelic self is certainly good for improving your everyday life and overall health and happiness. However, it's also a fabulous way to cultivate your ability to achieve the flow state during rituals. You know how they say "practice makes perfect"? Well, this is one of those situations where the more you do something, the easier it becomes.

Your goal during ritual shouldn't be to fall into a flow state. Instead, the flow state should be the vehicle by which you enact the ritual and its purpose. If you try too hard, you're going to end up frustrated; remember that two of the key parts of flow are a loss of self-consciousness and a lowering of the ego. In order to flow, you have to learn to let go.

Start off by consciously designing your ritual and its setting. Think about the most successful rituals you've ever been in. What do you think made them work so well for you? Was it the setting itself, or who you were with (even if that was just yourself)? What

activities in the ritual really clicked for you? Or was it the ritual's purpose that compelled you the most? Take note of these, because those may be some of the best things to help trigger flow.

Next, think about the times in your life you've achieved flow. What made that happen? Was it the activity itself or the setting? Maybe you were a child who had few responsibilities, and you felt more free to let yourself fall entirely into your interests. Do your best to identify the common themes among these various flow experiences you've had, and see how they might compare to the list of traits that made your best rituals as effective as they were.

Now, how can you make use of these factors in your ritual design? Let's say, for example, that crafting something with your hands helps you to get into the zone, so to speak. You might make creating artwork part of your ritual; it doesn't have to be anything big and elaborate. Or if movement is key to your flow states, make sure that you have some kinesthetic elements in your ritual. Don't worry if there are some things you can't access right now; just work with what is possible and shelve the rest for later.

When you're setting up the ritual space, pay attention to the sensory cues you're giving yourself. There are very good reasons that so many books and other guides on ritual craft tell you to pick colors, scents, music, and other sensory stimuli that are associated with the intent of your ritual or the deities or other beings you will be calling on. Each one of those stimuli is a trigger for your mind to help you get into the right headspace, both consciously and otherwise. Again, think back to the most effective rituals you've participated in and what sensory elements may have stood out to you the most. Make use of those as best as you can.

Being in the Flow

Now it's time for the ritual itself. First, and most importantly, you want to do everything you can to make sure you won't be disturbed. That means putting your phone on silent, asking anyone else sharing the space to give you some peace and quiet (as much as possible, anyway), and even putting a Do Not Disturb sign on any doors. However, you also need to make sure you won't be disturbing yourself with mental chatter and worries, which may necessitate some meditation or other relaxing activity to get started.

Pay special attention to the preliminary setup just before the ritual itself. For me, changing into my ritual garb is one of the most important cues. Like Mr. Rogers taking off his jacket and putting on one of his cozy sweaters, changing from everyday wear to ritual wear is a signal that Something Is Different. It's always been that way for me, whether it was putting on my uniform for track and cross country meets in high school or wearing my name badge when leading volunteer crews for habitat restoration activities.

Whatever your cue is, allow it to put you in that liminal space where anything is possible and the ordinary becomes the extraordinary. This allows you to become open to many possibilities, rather than the well-worn routes of your everyday life. It also lowers self-consciousness by letting you become the best version of yourself for this purpose; you shed your doubts and worries and become that magical being you know you are deep down inside.

Now: forget about flow. Just focus on the ritual. Let yourself be inspired; even if you had a carefully crafted plan, don't panic if you find yourself compelled to go off script. Do what feels the most right in the moment, and let the energy and the beings you are working with guide you along. This doesn't mean losing all control; rather, it's a process of letting your instincts and intuition guide you, all while still paying keen attention to the purpose and goal your ritual is heading toward.

If you find yourself suddenly jarred out of flow, don't panic and *don't feel bad that you couldn't keep it longer.* It's unpleasant and probably frustrating that you were interrupted, but be glad you got to that state in the first place! It means it's something you're still capable of, and remember that the more you practice the better you'll get. I leave it up to you to decide whether you're willing and able to try to get back into it, or whether it's time to close up the ritual and give yourself some time to transition back to your everyday state.

By actively caring for your autotelic self and consciously cultivating the flow state in your life, you're doing yourself a world of good, both during rituals and in your everyday life. Doing things for their own sake removes the frustration of external rewards and allows you to more fully immerse yourself in the experience. (And any extrinsic effects just become additional bonuses!) Even if you were to never practice another ritual again, the benefits that would weave throughout your life are worth this endeavor in and of themselves. May the flow be with you!

Further Reading

Csíkszentmihályi, Mihály. *Finding Flow: The Psychology of Engagement with Everyday Life.* New York: Basic Books, 1997.

———. *Flow: The Psychology of Optimal Experience.* New York: Harper Perennial Modern Classics, 2008.

Letting Go of the Moon: Embracing Elder Energy after Menopause

Monica Crosson

"Welcome to menopause!" A friend raised a glass of wine to me during an evening visit when I expressed my concerns that I just might have dementia, due to several bouts of "fuzzy thinking." "How's your moon cycle been?" she asked.

"Becoming scant." I swallowed the last of the contents of my glass. "I expected hot flashes, not insanity." I chuckled.

"It's different for everyone. I sweat through my sheets every night for a year," she said. "My vagina dried up and I had to start making lists."

"Oh God." Within my overactive imagination, flashes of a shriveled prune between my legs emerged. I shivered.

Growing up, *menopause* was a word whispered between women in my family of a certain age. These women, who teetered around my grandmother's kitchen, were strange creatures who wore permanent pressed polyester pants and childish printed sweatshirts with faux lace collars, and all of them wore hairstyles perfectly helmeted around their faces. I looked to them as old women, cranky and secretive (though they were most likely younger than I am now). I made a promise to myself not to be become like them, then solidified it by making a pact with my sister. "If I ever come to a point in my life when I perm my hair close to my head, wear permanent pressed pants, or a sweatshirt with a lace collar," I said, "you must shoot me on the spot."

"Deal," she said.

It wasn't until I was in my early twenties that I met a woman by the name of Stella, who I have talked about in both of my books. Though she was older than both of my grandmothers, she was strong, confident, and not afraid to express her truth. She had wild hair, long and pulled into a messy bun, that more times than not had bits of moss or twigs tucked in here or there. She taught me most of what I know about gardening, wildcrafting, and magick. She was healer, an activist, an artist, and a Witch in every sense of the word. She called herself a crone. It was through knowing her that my fear of growing old dissipated, and I knew I would welcome the stages of wisdom and wild.

The Changing Faces of the Triple Goddess

The Triple Goddess reflects the phases of the Moon (or seasons) and symbolizes the phases of life. Maiden is the waxing Moon (spring) and new beginnings—they are wonderment and enthusiasm for whatever they choose to manifest. They are vivacious and social and ready to take on the world. The Mother represents the Full Moon (summer) and a warrior spirit. They are empowerment and fertility (whether they choose to be a literal parent or to birth ideas and ripen new opportunities). They nurture everything they touch to fruition. The Crone is represented by the waning Moon (winter) and personifies wisdom. It is this phase that moves effortlessly between the worlds. They move beyond the realm of self, for they are confident in their power.

To be completely honest, as a woman somewhere in her fifties, I wasn't sure if I was ready to consider myself a crone. Some consider the transition to elder (crone phase) beginning thirteen months after one's last moon cycle; others say two years. Astrologically, it is suggested that a croning rite be performed during Saturn's second return in one's life (58 to 60). I have been to rites of passage where an elder transitioned in their seventies and to a few

where the celebrant was in their forties. This makes sense since life expectancies were much shorter at one time.

But in the past several years, a new phase has been added, and it was this phase that resonated with me. The *Maga* (meaning magician) phase has been placed between that of Mother and Crone and reflects the autumn season of life, representing those in their late forties to early sixties. The maga are comfortable in their own skin—they represent focus, intuition, and celebration. They allow themselves healing and acceptance and long to share their unique gifts. For women in this phase of life, menopause is real, and its symptoms are no joke. But the maga, unlike their grandmothers before them, no longer repress their natural energies and emotions that come with this transition.

Dealing with the "M" Word

Menopause is the end of a woman's Moon (menstrual) cycle and happens when the ovaries are no longer making estrogen and progesterone. It is a transition that occurs in three phases, and the symptoms that we associate with menopause, which can range from extremely mild to severe, actually occur in the first stage known as perimenopause. Perimenopause crept into my life around the age of fifty. That's when my moon cycle became erratic—light flow one month, followed by an excessively heavy flow to no flow at all. Other symptoms that plagued me were fuzzy thinking, irritability, and weight gain. But fluctuations in hormones may also cause hot flashes, vaginal dryness, racing heart, headaches, trouble sleeping, sweating, lower sex drive, and painful sex. The average length of perimenopause is approximately four years.

It is important during this time to eat a healthy, nutrient-rich diet, get plenty of exercise, and try to limit your intake of caffeine. Allow yourself the luxury of self-care. Practice meditation, yoga, and mindfulness. Take long walks along the beach or in your favorite park. Learn a new skill or take up an old hobby you loved before life became too busy. And guess what? It's okay to grieve for the loss of that cycle that synchronized so well with that of the Moon's own waxing and waning. I remember when the realization that menopause was really happening and I was close to losing my own cycle hit me. I went out and stood under a Full Moon near the edge of the river and wept. I threw rocks and yelled at the universe. When I was done, I felt better. A relief washed over me, and I was soon able to embrace the natural rhythms of my body and found a new freedom.

Menopause is the second phase of the menopausal transition, and this occurs when your moon cycle has been absent for twelve months. This indicates the end of one's reproductive ability. But it's not over yet, folks. You may continue to experience mild symptoms due to the decrease of hormones. On the next page you will find a list of herbs that may help ease your symptoms and an herbal tea recipe that I consider a warm hug from nature.

Postmenopause is the third phase of the menopausal transition, and it happens from menopause to the end of a person's life. One may still feel a few symptoms, but they tend to dissipate completely for most women within a couple of years. For our ancestors, this was the beginning of the end (thanks to lower life expectancy). Nowadays, a healthy woman may enjoy nearly as many years of life after menopause as she did before it. So celebrate your new freedom!

Letting Go of the Moon

This simple ritual may help you embrace your own changing body as it transitions through the phases of menopause. Do this ritual during one of your waning menstrual cycles.

You will need:
Black candle
Small amount of your menstrual blood

Anoint the black candle with the blood. Play a favorite piece of music, light some incense, and make yourself comfortable. As you light the candle, thank your body for its natural rhythms. Reflect on the good, the bad, and the ugly that came with having a menstrual cycle. Don't be afraid to laugh out loud or to weep hot, angry tears. Remember, your body serves you well and knows when it's time to transition. Allow the candle to burn out. Allow yourself to accept your new phase.

Herbal Support for Menopause

Black Cohosh: May help to reduce vaginal dryness and hot flashes.

Ginseng: May help reduce the occurrence and severity of hot flashes and night sweats.

Green Tea: Strengthens bone metabolism and helps decrease the risk of bone fractures, especially in people experiencing menopause.

Lavender: May help ease mood swings and help with sleeplessness.

Licorice Root: May reduce the occurrence of hot flashes for those entering menopause. It may also have estrogen-like effects.

Red Raspberry Leaf: May lessen heavy menstrual flows, especially those that come at the onset of perimenopause.

Red Clover: May ease hot flashes and night sweats.

Rose: May ease the symptoms associated with menopause, cramping, and mood swings.

Valerian: May help with sleeplessness, anxiety, headaches, and stress.

Love Me Gently Tea
2 parts raspberry leaves
1 part rose petals
½ part dried ginger
½ part ground licorice root
½ part black cohosh root

Place the tea in a tea ball and let it steep in hot water for approximately 5 minutes. Enjoy with a little honey.

Welcome Autumn

They are the wise women, the elders, the hag queens, the witches whose status, wisdom, beauty, and power deserve celebration. Being a modern crone or maga is no longer stigmatized with the image of an unattractive shrew who has lost their feminine prowess due to age. The modern elder shakes off their fears and steps into their power. People are drawn to them for their courage, knowledge, and beauty that only comes with self-assurance.

I was lucky enough to place a crown of woven grass on one of my best friends, who used her seventieth birthday as the platform

for her croning ceremony. Together, we planned the ritual and wrote the script (which is important—and that is why I didn't include a script in the ritual below). I stood at the quarter of autumn and cried as she handed me a lovely black dyed egg she lovingly scratched with words of wisdom and power. It was a magickal experience for us all.

An elder blessing ceremony empowers the celebrant by affirming their attainment of wisdom. It allows for reflection and to be honored for this important transition in one's life. So, whether you're seventy with your feet firmly planted in elderhood or you are have just completed menopause and are feeling drawn to crone (or maga) energy, here is the outline of a ceremony you might consider. This outline is specifically for a croning blessing, but you can revise it for a maga, elder, wise woman, and so on.

You will need:
Garments in traditional colors for a croning ceremony: black, silver, and purple (But of course, the celebrant is free to choose whatever colors they like.)
Lit cauldron
3 blown eggs, dyed black, that the celebrant will use a candle scribe to scratch words of wisdom on for each of the individuals involved in the ceremony
Gifts: maiden to present a cord, mother to present a shawl, maga to present a crown
Twig from a tree associated with each phase (e.g., alder for maiden, oak for mother, ivy for maga, and elder for crone)

Group members representing the phases of maiden, mother, and maga will use besoms to clear negativity from sacred space. The crone will take their place in the center of the circle near a lit cauldron. The maiden will take their place in the circle at the eastern quarter (representing spring). The mother will take their place at the southern quarter (representing summer), and the maga will take their place at the west (representing autumn). Call the quarters in your own way.

The celebrant will begin at the eastern quarter, where they are welcomed by the maiden, who offers the celebrant a gift in exchange for wisdom. Words that are exchanged may be scripted or allowed to flow organically. The crone will hand the individual the black dyed egg that has been scratched with messages especially for them. The maiden will assist with the tying of the cord around the celebrant's waist. As the celebrant makes their way (deosil), they will stop at both the southern and western quarters, where the process is repeated.

After the maga crowns the newly born crone, the representatives of the corners will move around the lit cauldron, inside which they will place their twigs. They all join hands and raise them skyward. Hail the Crone!

Sabbath
Guided Meditation
Kelden

Perhaps one of the richest bodies of folklore regarding Witchcraft is that pertaining to the Sabbath. Emerging in the early modern period, the Witches' Sabbath was said to be a nocturnal gathering of Witches and their leader, the devil. The concept of the Sabbath has no clear, singular point of origin. Instead, it grew across time and space, like a creeping vine, twisting together both ecclesiastical ideology and earlier pagan folk beliefs. At these supposed nighttime conventicles, Witches were said to work magic (typically to harm their enemies), feast, dance, make music, and engage in sexual acts. Throughout the European and American Witch trials, these stories were colored by regional and cultural details. For example, in areas closer to the Holy Roman Empire, Sabbath stories commonly featured highly ceremonial elements as a direct inverse of the Christian Mass. Meanwhile, in places like Scotland, stories of the Sabbath were much more focused on revelry and merriment.

During the modern Witchcraft revival (mid-twentieth century), the Witches' Sabbath re-emerged in two distinct ways. First, through the work of Gerald Gardner (who was highly influenced by the writings of Margaret Murray), the Witches' Sabbath became a set of seasonal celebrations. Today we know these *sabbats* (Gardner preferred the French spelling of *Sabbath*) as the Wheel of the Year. Within Wicca and broader Neopaganism, these holidays are used as both a narrative of the Mother Goddess and Horned God and a way in which to connect with the seasonal tides. At the same time, though, the Witches' Sabbath was being approached by certain occultists—

specifically Austin Osman Spare as well as Kenneth and Steffi Grant—as an otherworldly gathering of Witches and spirits through which spiritual gnosis could be attained and acts of magic wrought. Sometime later, occultist Andrew Chumbley would take the work of his predecessors and forge a tradition based in the imagery of these otherworldly meetings, known as the *Cultus Sabbati.*

In the practice of Traditional Witchcraft, we approach the Sabbath in the same way that Chumbley did. It is a spiritual event, taking place in realms beyond our own physical one. It is here where we can meet with spirits, make pacts, work magic, and engage in ecstatic revelry. In order to journey to the Witches' Sabbath, practitioners engage in the practice of spirit flight. This process involves the spirit leaving the physical body behind and traveling into the otherworld, wherein the Sabbath can be found.

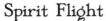

Spirit Flight

A common question I get in regard to the art of spirit flight is how it differs from guided meditations. I would say that the difference lies in the location of the work being done. When engaging in guided meditation, you are working within yourself, within your mind and body. On the other hand, while in spirit flight, you are working outside of your physical form. That being said, guided meditations and imagery can be useful leading up to the point at which one's spirit travels forth, especially for beginners. Utilizing a guided meditation helps give a framework for building one's journey, allowing it to unfold organically from that point on. For those who are new to the concept of the Witches' Sabbath, guided meditation can also help one become familiar with its key imagery.

The following meditation uses visualization, but I'd like to take a moment to discuss what exactly this means. Although the word *visualization* includes the word *visual*, when I use the term, I am not strictly referring to ocular imagination. Instead, I think of visualization as imagination utilizing any of the five senses. Many people, including those with aphantasia, are unable to picture images within their mind. However, they may be able to imagine sound, touch, taste, or smell. You may be able to imagine with all your senses, a combination of a few, or only one in particular. Practice and see which of your imaginative senses are strongest. Practice those that may need improvement, but know that you are not barred from this work simply because you cannot see images within your mind.

Preparation

Before we begin, let's take a moment to focus on our breath. Specifically, we will be utilizing a technique known as box breathing. To start, take in a nice, deep inhale through your nose. As you breathe in, feel your stomach expanding outward. Hold your breath for just a moment or two and then exhale fully. As you exhale, feel your stomach flatten back down. Hold your breath once more, for just a moment or two, before starting the process over again. And so it goes: inhale, hold, exhale, hold, repeat. It's important for you to allow your breath to come naturally. Don't force yourself to inhale, hold, or exhale for any longer than what is comfortable. Once you get the hang of box breathing, you can move on to the meditation itself.

To prepare for the meditation, you may wish to memorize the prompt. You can also have someone read it to you or record yourself reading it and then play it back when ready. Additionally, you'll want to prepare your space by limiting distractions, especially noise. Turn off your phone and tell others not to disturb you for the time being. You may want to prepare the space magically by lighting some candles (please practice fire safety) and incense, or even laying a compass or casting a circle. Once your space is ready, sit down or lie down, making sure that your body is comfortable. Close your eyes and begin box breathing.

Sabbath Meditation

You find yourself standing before an unlit hearth. The clock on the mantle ticks closer to the midnight hour, and your heartbeat quickens with anticipation. You pull out a small vial of greenish oil, uncap it, and take an inhale. It has a rich, herbal aroma. With skilled fingers, you apply a thin layer of oil to your wrists, feeling it glide coolly against your skin. Grabbing the ancient broomstick resting against the hearth, you speak secret words of power, hearing them ring out as the clock strikes the hour. With a sudden whoosh, you are carried up the smoky chimney and out into the cold night.

The chilly night air whips around you as you speed across the dark sky. The rush of the wind fills your ears with the sound of freedom and promise of the magic to come. Further on you go, out of your town and into the untamed wilderness beyond. Finally, you come to a stop above a clearing in a dense pine forest. With another whoosh, you find yourself standing firmly upon the ground, feeling the solid earth beneath your feet.

The sight before you is one of archaic awe and thrilling excitement. In the center of the clearing, a bonfire blazes with intensity, sparks shooting up into the sky. Your ears are met with the sounds of a haunting tune played by Witches on various instruments. Drums. Fiddles. A tambourine. Filling the forest with an eerie melody to which masked attendees dance. They spin widdershins around the bonfire, arms locked with backs to the flames. You hear these Witches shouting and singing, their strange, barbarous words stirring something deep and primal within you. Moving on, you find yourself standing before a banquet

table laden with an abundance of food and drink. You pick up a stoneware cup and take a sip, tasting a rich red wine on your lips. The smell of roasted vegetables and sweet cakes wafts around you, leaving you with hunger in your stomach.

Toward the edge of the clearing, you spot Witches at work, some crushing plants in a mortar and pestle, some fashioning small poppets from wax, and others tying knots along thick cord while whispering secret words. These workings, they tell you, are for both blessing and bane, for the Sabbath above all else is a place of transgression and personal sovereignty. You notice too that not all the attendants appear to be of the physical realm. There are ghosts from ages long past and faeries too who have come out from their mounds for this special occasion. Together, the Sabbath guests weave magic, celebrate, and make mischief.

At the northern point of the clearing, you stop in front of two seated figures. The first is a goat-headed man. Between his horns is a lit candle, burning with a brilliant light. Beside him is a woman dressed in white with long black hair and a silver crown upon her head. You know immediately that they are of great importance. They are the Witch Father and Witch Mother, the Man in Black and the Sabbath Queen. It is they who preside over the gathering, who share their wisdom and power with those in attendance. They work to inspire, empower, and embolden. They nod to you, and you feel the continued awakening of a primordial power within your very core.

"Be free," they speak, their words echoing through the woods, through your soul.

Now is the time to dance, to feast, to make magic. Give yourself over to the wilderness of the Sabbath and be free.

At this point, allow the meditation to unfold organically. When you are ready to move on, continue as follows:

With a start, you are brought to your senses by the crowing of a rooster. The music stops abruptly, and the entire assembly stops dead in their tracks. Without another moment's notice, Witches begin to take to the sky. You can see through the trees that the Sun is beginning its

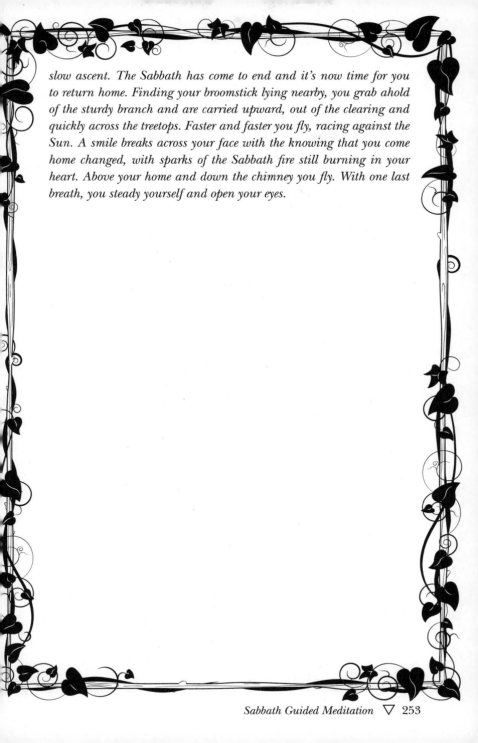

slow ascent. The Sabbath has come to end and it's now time for you to return home. Finding your broomstick lying nearby, you grab ahold of the sturdy branch and are carried upward, out of the clearing and quickly across the treetops. Faster and faster you fly, racing against the Sun. A smile breaks across your face with the knowing that you come home changed, with sparks of the Sabbath fire still burning in your heart. Above your home and down the chimney you fly. With one last breath, you steady yourself and open your eyes.

Balance

Daniel Pharr

S taying centered and focused is probably the most important aspect of witchery. Learning to stay focused while maintaining emotional balance is an art that will pay dividends not only in the otherworld of magic and mysticism, but in the mundane world as well. People are expected to have a calm demeanor in the face of incredible turmoil. When the expectation is met, the person is believed and considered to be truthful. When the person loses composure, the person is considered irrational and not to be trusted. Perception is everything.

At first look, staying centered and focused might feel like an elemental matter for an air-based ritual or possibly earth. However, when in need of solid, deep-to-your-bones grounding, start with water. Sure, the very term *grounding* associates the process with the earth, and the idea of "focus" must be an airy activity. But water

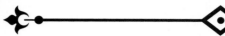

washes the psyche, clears the issues from distraction, and hydrates the being.

I was once interviewed by an investigator looking into the suicide of a colleague. My colleague and I had interacted only days before. I was nervous on many levels, worried what I might be asked or say, what the investigator might think, even that I was somehow responsible, like I should have told someone of my colleague's erratic behavior.

I went back to my training. In times of crisis, going home is often the answer. Home, in my case, is my early training at Our Lady of the Shining Staar. Balance is achieved in steps, adding layers of support and protection throughout the process.

Every element has sub-elements. Earth is not just earth, but a combination of all four elements—earth, air, fire, and water—and the same can be said of the other elements. Fire is the simplest example of the interactions, as fire is totally controlled by earth, air, and water. For fire to even exist, wood (earth) and oxygen (air) are necessary in the proper ratio, and the presence of water controls how hot the fire burns or even if fire burns at all. Each sub-element is also made up of the four elements in varying degrees. This level of detail can be extended deeper and deeper to a minute microscopic depth if desired. Generally, the first or second level of elemental action will provide all the vital demands and support needed for most rituals.

The following rites will aid you in finding balance and preparing for a challenge ahead.

Sacred Salt Bath

Salt baths are a part of my spiritual rejuvenation, and I soaked before my interview. The easiest of all cleansing and centering magical acts is the salt bath—a long, hot soak with a handful of sacred salt dissolved within. Soak the whole body in the bath for as long as feels right.

Sacred salt can be had as easily as saying a blessing over a bowl of salt (preferably kosher salt because it has no additives) or can be created and consecrated in ritual, as described here:

Sacred Salt Recipe

Cold seawater, clean is the best,
Gather in jugs once Moon is crest.
Cancer Full Moon, time opportune,
Or waxing Cancer, never June.
Through towel pour seawater, strain.
Rest the water, settle remains,
Sedimentation, forgotten.
Siphon water into cauldron.
Boil, boil, bubble, toil
That remaining looks like wet soil.
Evaporate in trays of glass,
Wet sand becoming salt at last.
Suspend damp salt in bags of cloth,
Drying away from flies and moths.
When dry as bones and brittle too,
Grind salt and store in bottles blue.

When setting up for a sacred salt bath, candles make a wonderful addition, providing heat for the surrounding air, subdued lighting, and magical assistance if preferred. Scenting the air also offers secondary succor. I always prefer unscented candles, as they provide for better control of the magical act. The scents sometimes comingle with the energies and skew the outcome. Of course oils or herbs can be added to a soaking bath, but since the idea with the cleansing bath is to capture and drain emotional maladies from the body, sacred salt is best allowed to do its job on its own. Just like salt draws moisture from meat and veggies, so does salt draw from the body.

When preparing the bath, recite the following:

Blessing a Salt Bath

Blessed water, element of west,
Infused by fire, the needed zest.
Sacred salt, of earthy helm,

Dissolve into water's realm.
Salt and water and waves of heat,
Earth, fire, water, elixir complete.
Draw from my body maladious intent,
That not serving me, to safety's extent.
Leave me calm and balanced, that's the key.
As is my word, so mote it be.

Remember to take this bath alone and allow no one to join. Do not let familiars or pets drink or dabble in the water. Drain the water as soon as the bath is done, and rinse the tub. The bathing water will be holding the negativity that was once in the body, and contact with another could cause them to absorb the negativity.

There have been discussions around collecting and weaponizing the remnants of clearing baths and other similar rituals, but the energies would be difficult to control and could have an effect other than what was desired. And then there is the rule of three to consider.

Clearing the Mind

Coming into contact with something unusual helps shift the mind from its worries to the unusual. This is the basis of tying a thread around a finger in order not to forget something. The thread is not supposed to be there, so its presence is a curiosity. The mind shifts to *Why is thread on my finger?* and then almost always knows the answer immediately: *I need to pick up bagels on the way to work.* This same exercise can be accomplished in a multitude of ways, like placing a dining room chair in the middle of the living room, putting the favorite coffee cup by the front door, setting the car keys in the refrigerator next to the coffee cream, dropping one shoe in one bathroom and the other shoe in another bathroom, putting a beach ball in the car seat. Anything unusual to jog the memory. In this case the memory will be to focus and center. Before stepping into the bath or going to bed, hide the car keys and shoes or anything that is worn daily in a place that is completely unexpected.

The next morning, recite a searching spell while retrieving the keys and shoes:

When I find my keys, I will not care,
Waves of sedition in the air.
Searching for keys and shoes in kind
Sweeps the worry from my mind.
I am focused, I am clear,
All day long, this atmosphere.

While sleeping, place any magical jewelry that is worn regularly or carried in a pocket, such as a pentacle, bracelet, or crystal, in a bowl of sacred salt. The salt, like the bath, will draw negativity that has been collected. Every emotion the wearer experiences has infused into the jewelry. Make a regular habit of jewelry maintenance and ground any jewelry worn, publicly, privately, or ritually, in salt to clear energies the jewelry will have absorbed.

When placing the pentacle, or any other jewelry or items that are worn or carried as personal magical protection, in the salt bowl while sleeping, as I did the night before the meeting, be sure to surround the body with protection. A trail of sacred salt circling the bed is my favorite.

To make a protective circle, say,

Let nothing less than good enter herein.

Envision a dome of protection at the salt circle delineation. Say,

Let no harm come to me or any being within the circle.

Visualize the dome receiving a bolt of protective energy. Say,

Sleep will come and sleep will leave.
Safe in the circle, so will I be.

Upon waking the next morning, place the jewelry in the freezer while preparing for the day. The purpose for wearing the cold jewelry against the skin is to remind the mind to remain cool and calm in the face of accusations and adversity. This is another version of the unusual. Slip the jewelry on just before leaving.

Dressing Rite

Donning clothing is much like donning armor. When putting on each piece of clothing, do so with the intent of armoring against an attack of any kind, mental, spiritual, emotional, or physical. The color of clothing and the coverage of the body is important. Color has many effects on the psyche. Colors that feel like strength and security, calm and balance, focus and freedom should be worn. Every time a sleeve or a leg drops into view, the color will remind the

wearer of its purpose. Body coverage should also be considered. Like armor, if a portion of the body is not covered with armor that same portion of the body is open to attack. Clothing was an easy choice for me: blue jeans and a white long sleeve button-up shirt, a heavy brown leather belt, and leather boots. Blue is a calming color for me and white is purity, unassuming and unblemished. The leather reminds me of armor and safety. The only exposure my body had was on the hands and head.

When dressing, recite,

Each piece of clothing worn today,
Regardless of for work or play,
Protects with earth, fire, air, and sea,
As is my word, so mote it be.

Eating Ritual

Eating is a grounding action. The intake of food sets a host of bodily functions into action, and the side effect of these functions is to bring the mind out of the clouds and into the moment of the mundane. Eating equals grounding, which is precisely why in most magical castings the magical practitioners fast prior to the ritual. Sometimes the fasting is for a few hours, for the day, or for several days, depending on the level and strength of energy being transmuted during the rite. (Speak with your primary care physician before undergoing any fasting regimen.) For my induction, I gradually reduced my food intake over the course of a month, and the last four days prior, I fasted. The reduced food intake and fasting, coupled with a sequence of clothing color choices and the elimination of certain words from my vocabulary slowly brought my body and mind closer to "pure," meaning unencumbered and focused.

However, for the meeting with the investigator, being grounded was the proper choice, so a full breakfast was needed, a breakfast that would stick with me. So I went back to my Irish roots and cooked a full Irish breakfast.

Driving Rite

Traveling from home to the office, school, shopping, or anywhere in the mundane world by mundane modes of transportation requires self-protection. Whether driving or riding, self-protection is mandatory. Raising shields around the traveler and the vehicle not only protects the people and parts, but it also inhibits psychic stalking. Drop a translucent ethereal bubble around the body, then around anyone else in the car, and then around the car. Recite the words below and envision the bubbles being charged with energy. Look around and actually visualize the bubble manifesting around the passengers and the car. Say,

May nothing less than good enter herein.
Let no harm come to me, this car, or its contents.
I conjure this spell, earth, air, land, and sea.
And as is my word, so mote it be.

Color Correspondences

Color magic uses various hues to influence energy. It can attract or repel, strengthen or weaken. It expresses thoughts and feelings that don't fit easily into words. People choose colors of clothes, jewelry, walls, and carpet to create desired effects. In magic, we use altar cloths, candles, gemstones, bowls, and other altar tools to channel this energy. Coloring pages help people relax.

Different cultures may use different correspondences. Western cultures associate white with life and black with death; Eastern cultures tend to reverse those. It comes from interpretations. Red is the color of blood, which can suggest vitality or danger, depending on how you look at it. So there is no "right" or "wrong" meaning. Use the color associations that resonate with you.

Maroon: Crone, drama, respect, sensuality

Crimson: Determination, righteous anger, survival

Scarlet: Action, female sexuality, vitality

Red: Fire, strength, danger

Orange: Creativity, addiction, opportunity

Gold: God, Sun, justice

Topaz: Male sexuality, memory, fast effects

Yellow: Air, joy, charm

Lime Green: Growth, speed, end frustration

Green: Envy, money, health

Teal: Acceptance, abundance, happy home

Turquoise: Work-life balance, guilt, receiving

Blue: Water, truth, family

Indigo: Will, spirit, psychic

Purple: Wisdom, emotions, power

Lavender: Knowledge, intuition, divination

Violet: Calm, gratitude, tension

Coral: Mother, nurturing, emotional energy

Pink: Love, compassion, partnership

Fuchsia: Fight depression, self-direction, self-worth

Rose: Maiden, romance, friendship

Brown: Earth, stability, memory

Tan: Construction, food, past life

Black: Dark Moon, defense, grounding

Gray: Balance, loneliness, rest

Silver: Goddess, Moon, dreams

White: Crescent Moon, purity, peace

Ivory: Full Moon, luxury, animal magic

Butterfly Coloring Spell for Transformation

Mickie Mueller

We're constantly transforming in life, shifting, changing, and reinventing ourselves. If there's one thing that's certain in life, it's change. Sometimes when we know that change is coming or needs to happen, it can be useful to guide things in the direction that we want with a spell.

A butterfly is a symbol of positive transformation: the caterpillar finds a safe, quiet space and creates a chrysalis out of its own body. Within the chrysalis, it breaks itself down and reforms itself. What we see in the end is a beautiful butterfly, but the process of getting there can be messy. It's important to remember that change isn't usually easy, but a good outcome is absolutely something that we can accomplish.

You will need:
White or yellow candle
Butterfly illustration on page 267
Colored pencils, markers, or any coloring tools of your choice

Light the candle and take a few deep breaths. Think about the transformation that you're undertaking and ask yourself, "What am I leaving behind in this transformation?" Focus on what felt safe in the past but no longer serves you as you color the chrysalis. You might wish to add colors that represent these things for you or color it in any way you wish, but be sure to focus on what you are shedding.

Next, think about the safest place in your world you know, your happy place. As you think about it, color the branch that supports the chrysalis. Think about your favorite crystals, the ones that make you feel safe, empowered, and strong. Color the three crystals as your favorite crystals; this has created your sacred nurturing space for change and growth.

Next, color the Moon phases above. They represent time and natural cycles of change. This is to remind yourself that change doesn't happen overnight. It will happen in its right time, so don't feel the need to rush. We need to always remember that we must work with the natural cycles of life to grow in healthy ways.

The flowers will be waiting for you when you break out of your transformation, so color them next. They will nourish you and your butterfly as you explore your beautiful new life, the new you. As you color the flowers and leaves, focus on allies and resources to help the transformation along, as the butterfly will feed from these flowers!

Now that everything is in place to help you with your transformation, you will color the butterfly, newly transformed, just spreading its wings in the warm air. As you color the butterfly, focus on your outcome. You can use colors that represent your goal or just do what feels right. As you color, think about how it will feel after the transformation, your goal achieved.

Now if you wish, you can color the rest of your world, where this butterfly will live. It's your world—create it! May the transformation you want for yourself and your life manifest beautifully!

Revelations Revealed:
Cauldron Magick

Monica Crosson

Imagine walking down a twisted trail where moonlight peeks between the branches of the bare trees that scratch at the sky. Whispering voices seem to stir the breeze and send shivers up your spine. As you reluctantly round a stony bend, you see three women nestled just inside the mouth of a cavern. Bent and gnarled with age, they cackle as they stir a giant black cauldron. "Double, double toil and trouble. Fire burn and cauldron bubble . . ." they chant. Your heart stills, for you know what bubbles and churns within their cauldron holds the power of revelation.

Of course, I am describing the scene in *Macbeth*, where he and his companion Banquo come upon the witches whose cauldron symbolized the turmoil he was yet to experience. Nowadays a black cauldron is synonymous with witches in black pointy hats, who, if not stirring up some trouble, can be found flying silhouetted across the Moon on Halloween night. Where did this image come from you may ask? Cauldrons are basically large metal kettles used to cook over an open fire. It is thought that their history goes back to the late Bronze Age. They were practical tools, found in almost any household, that held contents of sustenance and healing. As the witch craze of the Middle Ages spread throughout Europe, images of women stirring up toxic brews helped popularize the modern perception.

The cauldron has quite a few appearances in mythology. Perhaps one of the most famous of mythological cauldrons is that of the ancient Welsh goddess Cerridwen, whose Cauldron of Inspiration is connected to rebirth, magic, and wisdom. To modern Witches, it represents the Goddess and her womb, the process of transformation, revelation, and purification.

Cauldron of Revelation

As you look at the illustration of the Cauldron of Revelation on the next page, focus on what you seek to reveal within the tendrils of smoke. What ideas do you have stirring within you? Maybe it's a new business venture, going back to school, or taking on exciting challenges for self-improvement. Before you begin, mix up some Three Witches Incense.

Three Witches Incense Blend

2 parts dragon's blood resin (courage)
1 part mugwort (prophecy)
1 part sage (wisdom)

Use a mortar and pestle to grind the resin and herbs.

For this spell, you will also need art supplies of your choice, such as colored pencils, crayons, watercolor pencils, and so on.

Plan on doing this during a waxing Moon. Pull from her gentle energies those things you want revealed. Play favorite music and burn the Three Witches Incense Blend while coloring. Use a charcoal incense tab in a cauldron or firesafe container.

Enjoy the process and take it slow. Remember, revealing your truth isn't something that can be done while coloring with the kiddos or between errands.

As you color, focus on those things that have been bubbling within you. Attempt your skills at automatic writing as you color the tendrils of rising smoke. What flowed from your pencil? Maybe an idea you hadn't even thought of yet.

Contributors

ELIZABETH BARRETTE has been involved with the Pagan community for more than thirty-two years. She has served as managing editor of *PanGaia* and dean of studies at the Grey School of Wizardry. Her book *Composing Magic* explains how to combine writing and spirituality. She lives in central Illinois. Visit her blog *The Wordsmith's Forge* (ysabetwordsmith.livejournal.com) or website PenUltimate Productions (penultimateproductions.weebly.com). Her coven site with extensive Pagan materials is Greenhaven Tradition (http://greenhaventradition.weebly.com/).

MIREILLE BLACKE, MA, LADC, RD, CD-N, is a licensed alcohol and drug counselor, registered dietitian, and freelance health and nutrition writer from the Hartford, Connecticut, area. She has written numerous articles for Llewellyn's annuals since 2014. Mireille worked in rock radio for two decades before shifting her career focus to media psychology, behavioral health nutrition, and addiction counseling. She remains fascinated with the city of New Orleans, her beloved (and insane) Bengal cats, forensic psychology, music that would surprise you, and the works of Joss Whedon.

BLAKE OCTAVIAN BLAIR is a shamanic and druidic practitioner, ordained minister, writer, Usui Reiki Master-Teacher, and musical artist. Blake incorporates mystical traditions from both the

East and West with a reverence for the natural world into his own brand of spirituality. He is an avid reader, knitter, nature lover, and member of the Order of Bards, Ovates, and Druids. He lives with his loving husband in the New England region of the USA. Visit him on the web at www.blakeoctavianblair.com.

CHIC AND S. TABATHA CICERO are Chief Adepts of the Hermetic Order of the Golden Dawn as re-established by their mentor, Israel Regardie (www.hermeticgoldendawn.org). The Ciceros have written numerous books, including *Golden Dawn Magic, The Essential Golden Dawn, Self-Initiation into the Golden Dawn Tradition, The Golden Dawn Magical Tarot,* and *Tarot Talismans.* They have edited and enhanced several of Israel Regardie's classic texts: *The Middle Pillar, The Tree of Life, A Garden of Pomegranates, The Philosopher's Stone,* and *Gold: Israel Regardie's Lost Book of Alchemy.* Both are prominent Rosicrucians: Chic is currently Chief Adept of the Florida College of the SRICF, and Tabatha is Imperatrix of the SRIA (www.sria.org). The Ciceros also create custom-made hand-crafted Golden Dawn implements based on their original designs from the book *Secrets of a Golden Dawn Temple* (www.goldendawnshop.com).

MONICA CROSSON is the author of *Wild Magical Soul, The Magickal Family,* and *Summer Sage.* She is a Master Gardener who lives in the beautiful Pacific Northwest, happily digging in the dirt and tending her raspberries with her family and their small menagerie of farm animals. She has been a practicing Witch for thirty years and is a member of Evergreen Coven.

KATE FREULER lives in Ontario, Canada, and is the author of *Of Blood and Bones: Working with Shadow Magick and the Dark Moon.* She owns and operates White Moon Witchcraft, an online witchcraft boutique. When she isn't crafting spells and amulets for clients or herself, she loves to write, paint, read, draw, and create. Visit her at www.katefreuler.com.

SASHA GRAHAM is the author of *Tarot Diva, 365 Tarot Spreads, 365 Tarot Spells,* and *Llewellyn's Complete Book of the Rider-Waite-Smith*

Tarot. She is the editor of and contributor to *Tarot Fundamentals, Tarot Experience,* and *Tarot Compendium.* Her tarot decks include the *Haunted House Tarot* and *Dark Wood Tarot.* Sasha hosts *The Enchanted Kitchen,* a short-form magical cooking series for YouTube and Heyou Media's *Mobile. Mini. Movies.*

RAECHEL HENDERSON (Chicago, IL) is the author of *Sew Witchy* and *The Scent of Lemon & Rosemary.* She has been sewing professionally since 2008 and has traveled around the Midwest selling her handmade bags, skirts, coats, and accessories at various events and conventions. She maintains a blog at idiorhythmic.com and is on Instagram and Facebook. She writes about magick, creativity, living by one's own life patterns, her family, and books.

JD WALKER resides in North Carolina. She is an avid student of herbology and gardening. She wrote a weekly garden column for thirty years. She is an award-winning author, journalist, and magazine editor and a frequent contributor to the Llewellyn annuals. Her book, *A Witch's Guide to Wildcraft: Uncommon Magick with Common Plants,* was published by Llewellyn Publications in 2021. When not at the keyboard, she spends time in her own landscape, taking trips with friends, and with her nose buried in a book.

This is **JAMES KAMBOS**'s twenty-fifth year writing for Llewellyn Publications. He has written many articles about folk magic traditions, spell craft, and herbs. He's also an artist and has designed cards and calendars. A gardener, he raises a large variety of herbs and wildflowers. He lives in the beautiful Appalachian hill country of Southern Ohio.

EMMA KATHRYN (Nottinghamshire, UK) is a staff writer at *Witch Way Magazine, The House of Twigs* blog, *Stone, Root, and Bone* blog, the *Spiral Nature* blog, and Gods & Radicals. She has spoken at a number of UK Pagan events, including Magickal Women Conference in London, and she has been interviewed on *The Witch Daily Show* podcast.

KELDEN (Minnesota) has been practicing Traditional Witchcraft for more than a decade. He is the author of *The Crooked Path* and *The Witches' Sabbath,* and his writing has appeared in *The Witch's Altar, The New Aradia: A Witch's Handbook to Magical Resistance,* and *Modern Witch* magazine. Additionally, Kelden is the cocreator of the Traditional Witch's Deck, and he authors a blog on the Patheos Pagan channel called *By Athame and Stang.*

LUPA is an author, artist, and naturalist in the Pacific Northwest. She is the author of several books on nature-based Paganism, as well as the creator of the Tarot of Bones and Pocket Osteomancy divination sets. Her love of nature and her background in psychology both inform her creative work and writing. More information about Lupa and her works may be found at http://www.thegreen wolf.com.

VERNON MAHABAL is the founder and director of the Palmistry Institute in Los Angeles, CA. He combines both Eastern and Western astrological disciplines into his practice. He continues new research, particularly within the field of dermatoglyphics (fingerprint biometrics). He has written three best sellers on the subject: *The Secret Code On Your Hands, The Palmistry Cards,* and *Crossing* (Mandala Publishing Group). He has written articles for *Women's Day* magazine, First For Women, and the *NY Daily News.* He is the palmistry consultant for *Coast to Coast AM.*

MICKIE MUELLER is a Witch, author, illustrator, tarot creator, and YouTube content creator. She is the author/illustrator of multiple books, articles, and tarot decks for Llewellyn Publications and also has a jewelry line with Peter Stone and a statuary line with Sacred Source. Her magical art is distributed internationally and has been seen as set dressing on SyFy's *The Magicians* and Bravo's *Girlfriends' Guide to Divorce.* She runs several Etsy shops with her husband and fellow author, Daniel Mueller, in their studio workshop.

DANIEL PHARR writes from his home in the woods of the Pacific Northwest. Much of his Pagan training was at Our Lady of

the Shining Staar, a residential Pagan seminary in New Mexico. He held the station of High Priest at Our Lady of the Sacred Rose, under the auspices of the Aquarian Tabernacle Church in Washington, a Wiccan spiritual organization.

DIANA RAJCHEL is the author of *Urban Magick: a Guide for the City Witch* and *Hex Twisting: Counter Magick Spells for the Irritated Witch*. She splits geographic time between San Francisco, where she co-owns Golden Apple Metaphysical with her business partner Nikki, and Kalamazoo, Michigan, where she writes, teaches, reads tarot, and community builds with her romantic partner Synty and their children. She is about eight years behind in her sleep but hopes to catch up someday.

SUZANNE RESS runs a small farm in the Alpine foothills of Italy, where she lives with her husband. She has been a practicing Pagan for as long as she can remember and was featured in the exhibit "Worldwide Witches" at the Hexenmuseum of Switzerland. She is the author of *The Trial of Goody Gilbert*.

MHARA STARLING was born and raised in North Wales, on the Isle of Anglesey, and is a native Welsh speaker. Her interest in Paganism, Witchcraft, and magic started when she was very young. Mhara is deeply inspired by the folklore and legends of Wales. Her recent book, *Welsh Witchcraft: A Guide to the Spirits, Lore, and Magic of Wales*, explores the magical culture of her native land in depth.

ASTREA TAYLOR is an eclectic Pagan Witch and the author of *Air Magic* and *Intuitive Witchcraft: How to Use Intuition to Elevate Your Craft*. She blogs as Starlight Witch, and she wrote passages for *Witchology, Green Egg, Llewellyn's Witches' Spell-A-Day Almanac, Llewellyn's Magical Almanac, We'Moon, The Witch's Altar,* and *Llewellyn's Witches' Companion*. Astrea presents workshops and rituals both online and at festivals across the country. Learn more at AstreaTaylor.com.

CHARLYNN WALLS is an active member of her local community and a member of a local area coven. A practitioner of the Craft for over twenty years, she currently resides in Central Missouri with

her family. She continues to expand upon her Craft knowledge and practices daily. Charlynn shares her knowledge by teaching at local festivals and continuing to produce articles with Llewellyn Publications.

CHARLIE RAINBOW WOLF is happiest when she is creating something, especially if it can be made from items that others have cast aside. Pottery, writing, knitting, astrology, and tarot are her deepest interests. A recorded singer-songwriter and a published author, she is an advocate of organic gardening and cooking and lives in the Midwest with her husband and special-needs Great Danes. Visit www.charlierainbow.com.

STEPHANIE WOODFIELD has been a practicing Pagan for over twenty years, and is a devotional polytheist, teacher, and Priestess of the Morrigan. She is an organizer for several Pagan gatherings. A longtime New Englander, she now resides in the Orlando area with her husband, two very pampered cats, and various reptiles. She is called to helping others forge meaningful experiences and relationships with the gods.

NATALIE ZAMAN is the author of *Color and Conjure* and *Magical Destinations of the Northeast*. A regular contributor to various Llewellyn annual publications, she also writes the recurring feature Wandering Witch for *Witches & Pagans* magazine. When not on the road, she's busy tending her magical back garden. Visit Natalie online at nataliezaman.blogspot.com.

... ☽ ...

Notes

... ☽ ...

... ☽ ...
Notes

... ☽ ...